A1 GEORGE LOCKYER
TALES AND TRAILS DOWN UNDER

Kahuku

Publishing Collective

Tales and Trails Down Under

© George Lockyer 2023

Text design by The Design Dept.
Cover design by The Design Dept.
www.thedesigndept.com.au

Editing by Kahuku Publishing.

Photo acknowledgements: Page 20, David Peach; Pages 27, 29, John Williamson; Page 54, John Arnold; Pages 88, 90, Joyce Scobie; Pages 112, 114, Robin Coxson; Page 129, Marie Munkara; Page 190, Bruce Sharman; Pages 227, 229, 233, Hagen Stehr; Page 238, Hamish Cooper; Page 261, Brendon Nelson; Page 273, Martin Little

First published in 2020,
Reprinted in 2023 by
Kahuku Publishing
PO Box 149 Takaka
Tasman 7142, New Zealand
www.kahukupublishing.com

All rights reserved.
This book or any portion thereof may not be reproduced or used in any manner whatsoever without the express written permission of the author except for the use of brief quotations in a book review. All inquiries should be made to the author.

ISBN: 978-1-7386002-0-5

TALES AND TRAILS
DOWN UNDER

GEORGE LOCKYER

Kahuku
Publishing Collective

This book is dedicated to Rob 'Crocko' Croxson who passed away during the writing of it and whose life story appears between its covers. He was one of a kind.

CONTENTS

Waiting for Percy — 15
Black Dog Rider. David Peach — 20
Bush Balladeer. John Williamson — 27

Up the Coast — 35

Into the Outback — 47
Rural Trainer. John Arnold. — 53
Newspaper Editor. Colin Jackson — 61
Cattleman. Mick Seymour — 72

The Never Never — 81
Lady from the Bush. Joyce Scobie — 86
Bush Business Man. Tim Carter — 98

The North — 105
Opportunist. Robin "Crocko" Croxson — 111
Indigenous Writer. Marie Munkara — 124
White Ribbon Rider. Janette Mann — 134

Through the Kimberley — 141
    Postie Bike Rider. Richard Wilkinson — 155

Heading South — 163
    'The Sarge' — 176
    Meticulous Restorer. Bruce Sharman — 190

The Nullarbor — 209
    World Tandem Riders. Lloyd and Louis — 219
    Tuna Baron. Hagen Stehr — 227
    Motorcycle Journo. Hamish Cooper — 238

Into the Morning Sun — 245
    The Director. Dr Brendan Nelson — 261
    Iron Butt Rider. Martin Little — 269

Acknowledgements — 278

I don't know the number but I'm sure that thousands of motorcyclists have probably circumnavigated this wide brown land since A. Grady set off from Perth in October 1924 and completed the journey in the Spring of 1925. Back then it would have, of course, been a huge adventure and achievement. I met a few travellers doing 'the lap' on my ride, some on motorcycles, many Grey Nomads in their $150,000 rigs and a couple of lunatics on push bikes. I even heard of, though unfortunately never met, a young guy pushing a hand-made cart. Circumnavigation becomes a personal Everest for travellers, and for some almost an obsession. I had nourished the desire to ride around Australia since 1981 when I'd travelled around the huge country as a young bloke on Greyhound buses and hitching. I recall myself often gazing longingly through the window of bus or car whenever I saw a motorcycle go by, face pressed against the glass, envying the feeling of freedom that travelling on two wheels brings.

In this day and age there's nothing particularly adventurous about it. Somebody has probably crawled around on their hands and knees, pushing a threepenny-bit along with their nose, while reciting some religious mantra! It's just there and something I wanted to do.

INTRODUCTION

But adventure is relative – to a toddler, a walk around the park is an adventure.

As I discovered in the writing of my last book, *The Long and Winding Aotearoa*, it's really the people you meet along the way that make a road trip like this one so rewarding. Most of the interviews in this book were arranged many months in advance for obvious reasons but a few were well met and spontaneous and I'm very grateful for their participation.

Mired as most of us seem to be in this complex, 21st century world we've created, in the gloopy, clinging mud of domesticity and responsibility, this journey, of course, offered another chance to escape into the Never Never. And what better way than in the saddle of a motorcycle? According to Jerome K. Jerome, author of *Three Men in a Boat*, "It was a mistake for a man to get into a groove, and that unbroken domesticity cloyed the brain," and, "this aching monotony of life, these days of peaceful, uneventful felicity, they appall one!" The most precious thing available to us is, of course, time and I'd reached the age where there was far less of it ahead, than had gone before, and so to quote folk singer Tracey Chapman, "if not now, then when?"

Chapter One.
WAITING FOR PERCY

"Open wide, drive that mystery road"

Midnight Oil.

Sydney town is a huge, sprawling, iconic super city, growing 20 per cent faster than New York or London where I was born. I lived here in the inner suburb of Newtown for 14 years and both my kids were born here, before moving to New Zealand in 2003 for a quieter, more rural lifestyle. It's 4.8 million residents enjoy a wonderful, exciting, prosperous and beautiful city which has, I think, a very bright future. Others would, of course, like to share in its bounty, among them, a good chunk of the roughly 170,000 migrants who arrive in Australia every year. Sydney, named after Viscount Sydney who sent the first fleet here from the Old Dart in 1787, reached the status of a City in 1842 and hasn't looked back.

I arrive on a cool July evening and armed with my Opal card, soon indulge in a week-long orgy of reminiscing and catching up with family and friends. I re-visit old haunts and reflect on the busy years of hard work (laying bricks), paying off a huge (at the time) mortgage and bringing up two kids. It's also a frustrating time as I eagerly await the arrival of my bike which hopefully is sailing across

the Tasman Sea on the good ship *ANL EMORA*. My other frustration is the 2018 World Cup and a young England side's steady progress, a happy phenomenon I hadn't witnessed since Germany knocked us out on penalties in Italia 1990.

Before I leave, I'm able to watch England's World Cup dream come to an end at the hands of tiny Croatia in the Semi-Final, deserving victors in the end. The three lion's roar is reduced to a whimper, the young team lacking the skill to go any further. Youth, pride and passion are simply not enough. It's only a game, I tell myself as I sob into my flat white! Unfortunately, I can remember as a boy in London when we actually won the thing, so have endured 52 years of misery ever since. I console myself with the thought that I now won't have to get a tattoo of the three lions, a thing I'd rashly promised my kids if we'd won!

I'm staying at my wife's uncle's apartment in beautiful Darling Point in the affluent eastern suburbs. On another cool, sunny morning with the currawongs loudly singing, I wander down to Richie's coffee shop below where I'm to meet David. He's kindly agreed to talk to me and braved the rush hour traffic to ride across the bridge from the North Shore.

Black Dog Rider
David Peach

I greet David, CEO of the Black Dog Ride as he parks his BMW GS 1200 by the kerb and takes off his helmet. The Black Dog Ride is an Australian charity organisation whose aim is to raise awareness of a silent killer – depression. Since the first ride in 2009 it has raised millions for mental health programmes around the Nation. Steve Andrews founded the charity in response to the sudden suicide of his best mate's wife Anna.

After getting the coffees in I ask David, how he got involved in the organisation. "Well," he begins, sipping his cappuccino "I had a mate I grew up with – we knew each other from Grade 5. Most of our youth resembled an arms' race, first on bicycles, then on motorcycles – every year one of us would get something bigger and better and faster, and the other one would follow." David and his mate were extremely close, living their lives in parallel – they were both best man at one another's wedding. "Then at age 38 he killed himself," says David, "and I never saw it coming."

That happened in 1999 and David says that for the next 10 years he flip-flopped between mad and sad, "I was very cranky at him because he didn't reach out," he says.

Then in 2012 a journalist mate of David's invited him along on a Black Dog run, a day's ride on the Central Coast. It was the first charity ride he'd ever participated in. He says, "it opened a kind of release valve and allowed me to try and make some good out of my friend's passing."

From then on, David went on every Black Dog ride and in 2015 he took part in his first 'big one,' to Uluru and back. "Three days after that, I flew to New York and joined the first Black Dog ride across America. So, it was in that year that I realised that this was something I really cared about. In August and September of 2015, I rode almost 20,000 kilometres," he says. "That must have been very cathartic," I offer, and he nods in agreement.

Then, in 2017 Steve Andrews was forced to step down as CEO due to health issues, which sent the charity into some disarray. "Steve, like many riders in the charity was profoundly affected by the suicide or in his case, suicides of people close to him," David says. "Speaking with my fellow riders, I discovered that 95% of them had been affected by the suicide of a close friend or been affected by depression themselves."

We talk for a while about one of my best mates, Richard "Wilf"

Willis who took his own life in 1999 aged 40. At the time, he lived in London and I lived in Sydney. "Did you see it coming?" asks David and I tell him I didn't.

"In my friend's case it was a slow spiral," he continues, "he had a pretty tough life, but we kept any eye on him and he never gave any indication that he might take his own life. And I suppose that's the sinister thing about depression. Ultimately, it's a one on one battle – you against your demons or whatever triggers it. All the rest of us can do is hope, stand by, be there and try to get them some help."

It's evident that David is a very passionate and dedicated man and the cause is very close to his heart. "The biggest challenge of course is to reach out and ask for help," he goes on. "And most people don't do that."

"So, is that the main aim of the organisation, to get people to reach out?"

"Absolutely," he replies. "To make it OK to talk about depression. To give people the ability to make it all part of a person's general health. If you break a leg, there's no question, you go to the hospital. If you get sick, you go to see your doctor. But so many people who struggle with depression battle it alone. So yes, the whole idea behind the organisation is to bring depression out into the open. Starting conversations and making people aware that it's OK to ask for help." He pauses as he eats his croissant and I order more coffee. "'If you're not OK, that's OK' is a line borrowed from another charity but we're all working on the same problem just from a slightly different angle," he says.

I ask David if he thinks that the stereotypical image of the macho Aussie male might hinder men from admitting they have a problem. "I've never been asked that before George, but thinking about it, it probably doesn't help!" he replies.

The organisation tries to be as inclusive as possible as far as riders go. "Statistically," he says, "our average rider is a business owner, is 57 years old and rides a Harley Davidson, which is basically me, apart from the Harley. We are trying to encourage youth as they are disproportionately represented in the suicide figures. We also have

many women ride with us, so there's no gender bias."

The Black Dog Ride is registered with the Australian Charities Non-profits Commission and holds Deductible Gift Recipient status, which means they can issue a tax-deductible receipt which can by claimed against a person's tax. "By doing that we accumulate funds and historically have helped the Black Dog Institute (people often confuse our two organisations), Lifeline, Beyond Blue, Head Space and number of other charities." But that's now changing under David's stewardship as the Government has started to inject funds into the sector, allocating grants to the likes of Beyond Blue and Head Space in the last year or so. "There's more money in those grants," David says, "than we'd make in a few years, so we can now turn our attention to helping smaller grass roots mental health projects that can't get on the Government's radar."

One such charity the Black Dog Ride is helping currently is the Kidman Foundation, founded by actress Nicole's father Anthony, one of the great proponents of cognitive behavioural therapy in Australia. Kidman, psychologist, biochemist and academic sadly passed away in 2014 aged 75.

"He started what was the Health Phycology Unit of the University of Technology, which was recently re-named The Kidman Foundation," David explains, "they've recently rolled out a scheme in Western NSW which is a school-based mental health training programme. So, they're showing teachers how to deliver mental health training to students as part of their curriculum."

Black Dog Ride representation is very strong in Western NSW as David points out. "Rural areas are awash with mental health issues," he says, "and because everyone knows one another in these rural areas, the ripple effect is enormous." And I feel sure that with the continuing drought, depression will be on the increase in the bush.

"I carry the grandiose title of CEO, but I've only got a staff of five!" David laughs. "One of the extraordinary things about the organisation is the volunteer army that does the vast majority of the work. David has put in plenty of time as volunteer, in 2015, '16 and '17 organising the one-day ride in western Sydney's Penrith and the Central Coast ride in 2018. "This year (2018) we will put 8,500 riders on the road simultaneously in 41 locations around Australia," David proudly says. I raise my eyebrows and nod, acknowledging the amount of organising this would have involved. "On the Penrith ride this year, they stopped checking people in at 900. So, a ride of that size generates a lot of media attention, which is what we want."

Each rider pays $30 to enter and, says David the one-day ride generates most of the charity's income for the year. Merchandise is also sold on the day plus other fund-raising such as raffles. "If I can use the Central Coast ride as an example," David says, "the bowling club puts on a sausage sizzle, the riders buy breakfast and the club kindly donates the profits to us."

There are also secondary beneficiaries. On the Central Coast ride it was a local mental health project called Behind the Scene, who specialise in providing Post Traumatic Stress Disorder recovery training for first responders such as Police, Fire Brigade and Ambulance. These small charities, David points out, are too small to be noticed and receive funding and don't have a big enough presence to make money from community events.

"So, it's the day ride that keeps the door open," he says, "and funds the running of the organisation because like any business, we have salaries, rent, phone bills, accountants, etc."

Next year (2019) is the 10th anniversary of founder Steve Andrews' original ride around Australia where he raised over $34,000 on his 26-day, 15,000-kilometre trip. On the 26th July the Black Dog Ride will set off from Steve's starting point in Busselton in WA, to repeat that ride and David plans to ride all the way around.

Next month David will be driving the support vehicle on the Perth to Darwin ride. "I've never been to the north of WA and they needed a support driver, so I thought why not."

"Well maybe we'll bump into each other," I say as David dons his gear, fires up his BMW and heads back over the bridge to the office to organise the next ride.

I, like many others occasionally suffer from the Black Dog of depression. I blamed my father for a long time. Or flatly refused to recognize that I might have a problem. As though sitting in an armchair, staring at a spot on the wall, expressionless was normal behavior. Perhaps that's why I've always been a kind of stimulus junky. In my youth, I was like that Energizer battery man on the advertisement, never sitting still for five minutes in case the bad chemicals in my brain started to play up. Reading was fine, and I did it voraciously and still do for it proves a wonderful escape.

My wife Karen helped tremendously, as did bringing up kids. I remember going to a shrink about 20 years ago in Sydney. After an earnest chat where I tried to be brutally honest with the poor woman, I was ushered into a yellow-walled room where I sat on a comfy leather couch and wrote a letter to my dead father as instructed. To the accompaniment of whales singing from a CD player and the subtle whiff of scented candles I poured my heart out, damning him for his indifference and selfishness. Who can say if the visit to the shrink helped. I didn't go back.

By far the best remedy was travelling. And travelling on two wheels in particular, where the activity at hand required your utmost attention and as you and your machine found your rhythm, you struggled up out of the dark country of depression to find worries (and the Black Dog) disappear like the sun burning off the morning mist.

My Kawasaki KLR 650, nicknamed 'Percy' finally arrives and after arranging an exorbitant insurance policy I excitedly twist the throttle and leave Mainfreight's Botany depot. Next day, I park Percy on the pavement in Crow's Nest, say a silent prayer to the traffic warden Gods and enter Warner Music Australia's offices where my next interviewee is performing a couple of songs from his new album, *Butcherbird* for recording company staff. He's a national treasure – as Australian as an Akubra and a pair of dusty Blundstones, and as iconic as Uluru.

Bush Balladeer
John Williamson

I've been a huge fan of JW for many years and remember during tough times in Sydney when 'the recession we had to have' (as Paul Keating coined it) came along just as we'd taken out our first mortgage, his songs of a simpler life on the land were very comforting. He's a busy man, having just returned from a small tour of South Africa and I'm very grateful for the chance to meet him.

After John's well-received little performance, I chat with him in a conference room over a cold beer and I have to admit I'm a little bit nervous. I try to hide any sign of hero–idolatry as we shake hands and sit down. With his neatly trimmed beard he looks quite youthful for 72.

John's big break came in 1970 when he won the TV talent quest show *New Faces*, performing *Old Man Emu*, a "novelty" song he'd written the previous year.

"I remember working on the farm, putting the radio on a post and hearing myself singing *Old Man Emu* for the first time and thinking how old I sounded," he says in that familiar Aussie drawl.

"I was only 24 but I guess people thought I never got older because I sounded old in the first place."

Although that song went to No.1 it wasn't all beer and skittles and the early 80's were difficult for John, as he tried to build on that early success. "Yeah, *Old Man Emu* was the first song I ever wrote, and it did well, so I thought it was going to be easy, but it took another 16 years for me to make it after that."

I ask him about those early fallow years. "Well I suppose I wouldn't have made any more music if it wasn't for the New South Wales club scene, especially around Sydney," he says as he sips his beer. "A bad juggler or a bad comedian could have gotten a job, there were that many clubs putting on shows and they were a great breeding ground. But the most important thing for me was learning how to become a performer. In the clubs and little pubs, I did covers and gradually tried some of my own songs, developed my kick box, did my own lighting and sound and everything. Slowly and surely, I built up my act and started writing the *Mallee Boy* songs."

John's breakthrough album, and one of my personal favourites, *Mallee Boy* was released in 1986, peaked in the Top 10 and remained in the Top 50 for the next 18 months. It was also the inaugural winner of the Best Country Album at the 1987 ARIA Music Awards and Album of the Year in the Country Music Awards of Australia 1987. "I went out with one roadie on a trip through Central Australia, where I

wrote the album *Road Though the Heart*. I also wrote *Raining on the Rock* on that trip which ended up on *Mallee Boy*. And I think it was then, in 1986 that I realised that I could write good songs."

Since *Raining on the Rock* JW has written many other powerfully evocative songs of the Australian land, songs that can make the toughest farmer or drover cry into his beer. I ask him if it was a conscious effort to make his songs sound more *Australian* than others. "As Aussies," he says, "we were always discouraged to write our own songs. I remember people saying I shouldn't be doing my own stuff you know. But when I was doing the pub circuit I started doing my own songs and when I sang *Cootamundra Wattle* and saw people cry I realised it was worth it and stuck to my guns. But there were so many songs on *Mallee Boy* that basically made my career."

True Blue, also from that album has become something of an unofficial anthem, as well as a calling card for JW, who often closes a show with it (as he did here 30 minutes ago). John Singleton had approached JW and asked him to write a song to go with his TV programme of the same name that encapsulated what it meant to be a "fair dinkum" Aussie and John was happy to oblige and admits that he was very lucky.

"The song," he explains, "is all about what it means to be a good Australian, about looking after this great country. It's not about what colour you are or where you come from, it's about being a good person and looking after one another. I had no idea of the impact it would have when I wrote it for him but thank goodness for Singo. I'm lucky now that I often do a corporate thing where I get paid a fortune for singing two songs, *True Blue* and maybe *Waltzing Matilda*."

JW was a bit peeved when he discovered that Singo had used the song and John's image singing it, to promote white-goods for Harvey Norman. "I was in Mt Isa at the time and some mates rang me and asked if I knew that I was on an ad for Harvey Norman." JW then spent $60,000 to put an ad in the national papers, telling the public it was not his idea. "I was one of the few people who stood up to Singo, but we're good mates now," he says.

When *Mallee Boy* went multi-platinum, JW realized that he could have a career, writing songs about Australia and singing with an Aussie accent. "I knew," he says, "that I was on the right track and I could continue to write songs unashamedly about our country. Not many people these days write about rural things. And to me life out in the sticks is what makes us different to the rest of the world. Big cities are just big cities but it's the bush that makes us uniquely Australian. The big problem then, of course, was to come up with an album as strong as *Mallee Boy*."

Over the years JW has played at some very large and prestigious events such as the Gallipoli commemorations, Don Bradman Memorial, Bali Bombing Memorials, Steve Irwin Memorial, Wallabies matches and cricket events. He says the one that affected him the most was the Steve Irwin Memorial. "Well I knew Steve personally, so it was very emotional for me," he says, "I hid myself away in a tent before going on, so I didn't carried away with it all. I considered it wasn't my luxury to get emotional anyway, because there were plenty of people who were closer to him than me. But seeing his best mates carrying his swag and putting it on a truck, that was pretty hard to watch. I surprised myself that I got through it actually."

JW says that Steve Irwin was exactly the same in person in the flesh as he was on TV, "he was just a really enthusiastic person," he recalls, "and strong. You knew all about it, if he gave you a hug!"

As well as being a singer, song-writer, TV presenter and painter, JW is also an outspoken Republican and environmentalist, and has upset a few people in the bush over the years with his views – and songs like *Rip Rip Woodchip* and *A Flag of Our Own*. "I think I've probably gained more fans than them over the years," says John, "but surely we live in a free country and Australia is about saying what you feel and speaking your mind. I mean you could a get a bullet if you said something wrong about Putin. But I think people realise that what I say is from the heart as I truly love this county and anyone that's destroying it should be held accountable."

John Williamson hasn't supported many other artists during his long career. But back in the '80s he supported Johnny Cash, a true legend of the music industry, for two shows in Tasmania. I ask him about his memories of The Man in Black. "Although I felt a bit insignificant performing before him," he replies, "I think I went over pretty well though. I remember he wore high heels and he was taller than me anyway, so with his black coat he looked a lot like Darth Vader. And when he hit those lower notes you could almost hear the windows start to rattle."

"Did you have much contact with him?" I inquire. "I didn't talk to him much, but I spoke with the people around him and I almost got a song on his next album, but it didn't quite get there."

I then ask him what sort of music he listens to if he wants to relax. "I don't really listen to much music anymore," he replies. "It's a bit like people who live on the beach and don't do much swimming. But I've been influenced by the likes of Bob Dylan, Kris Kristofferson and Harry Belafonte. I was into Calypso music years ago and that kinda turned into Reggae and I love Bob Marley, especially if I'm drunk enough to dance," he laughs. "But I also like Frank Sinatra. Just good vocalists I suppose."

We talk for a bit about my favourite songs and how my son and I could both tear-up in the ute, listening to the likes of *Cootamundra Wattle* or *Galleries of Pink Galahs*. "Well, when I first write a song, I can well-up," he says. "that's when I know if I've got something or not. If I tear-up, then I think it's going to work."

"With all the lyrics you've written over the years, do you ever forget any of them?" I ask him. "Well, I can drift off on any song," he says. "You've just got to concentrate. Which is why I always have an afternoon nap before a show because it's your concentration that goes first, not so much your energy."

"Were you always an environmentalist?" I venture, changing tack.

"Well I suppose when I realised the harm we were doing, was when we moved up to north-west NSW. It was great soil so there was still a lot of clearing going on and it was inevitable that it was going to be cleared. But I started to object to *everything* being cleared. So, I started to say, 'hang on Dad, lets slow down a bit.' So that's where it began."

"Did he listen to you?"

"Yeah, he did. We could have ploughed the lot up, because it was all good country, but we left around 10% of it untouched. So, I've seen both sides of the coin. But the bush is so different from place to place and so much of it is being lost. People are wiping out whole, unique areas."

Despite this, JW is still hopeful about the future of the bush and thinks we have turned the tide, with initiatives from Bush Heritage Australia. Founded in 1990 by Dr Bob Brown the organisation strives for the long-term protection of the nation's biodiversity through the acquisition and management of land.

"There are a lot more people concerned now," he continues, "and a lot of forest has been saved from being felled for woodchip, and areas are being re-planted."

Unfortunately, my time with JW is drawing to an end and his manager pokes his head in the door, pointing to his watch and making signs. Finally, I ask him if he has a bucket-list. He ponders it for a while, "well I don't think I've got a bucket-list musically anymore, as I've gone much further than I expected to. I don't expect to write any more great songs. It may happen, but I don't worry about it. That's why the making of this new album *Butcherbird* was so relaxed because there was no pressure. I suppose I'd like to spend more time with my art.

I feel like a white Aboriginal I guess," he says. "If I can walk into a piece of virgin forest George, where perhaps no human's been before, then I feel privileged. The most important thing to me is nature. If we destroy it then we destroy ourselves really."

Chapter Two.

UP THE COAST

"Lord, I was born a ramblin' man."
The Allman Brothers

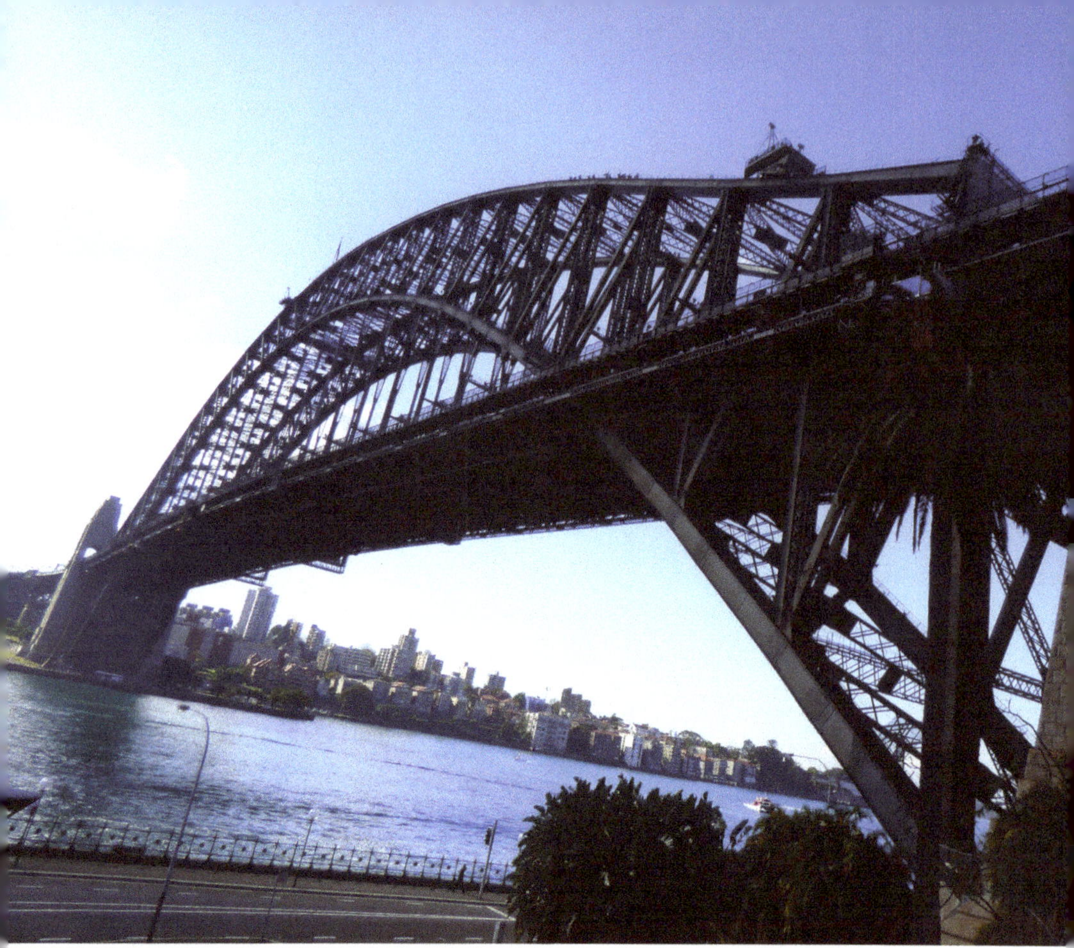

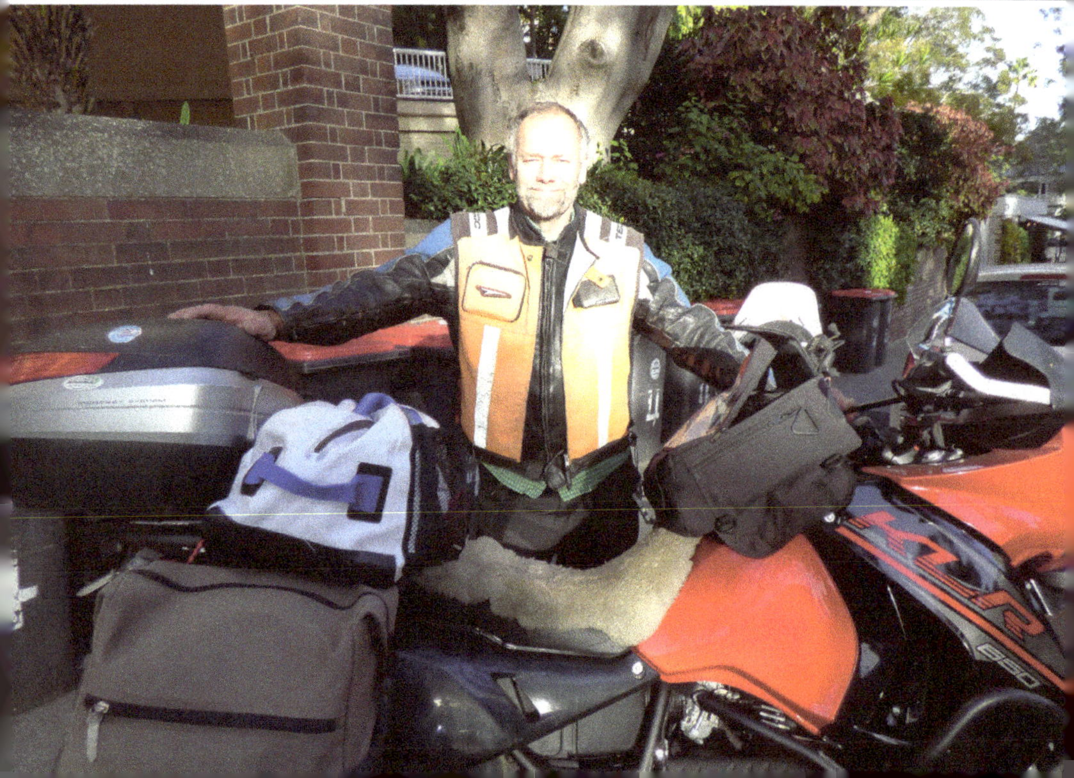

B idding farewell to Uncle Pete, I point Percy, not at the porcelain but north with the familiar fluttering of butterflies the beginning of any trip brings. It's hard to keep the grin off my face as I head the over the 'coat hanger', the Sydney Harbour Bridge in commuter traffic. Riding a motorcycle is when I feel most alive. You can be Don Quixote tilting at windmills, Clint Eastwood, in *High Plains Drifter*, Marlon Brando in *The Wild Ones* or Peter Fonda in *Easy Rider*. Take your pick.

Before construction was completed in 1932, horse-drawn carts, people and cars crossed the harbour by ferry which connected Dawes Point on the south side to Blues Point, the headland to the west of Luna Park.

The Aussie flag, so similar to the Kiwi one, flutters in the breeze. There is currently a political fight brewing over the suggestion that the Aboriginal flag have a permanent presence on the bridge, rather than its current 15 days per annum. Cheree Toka, a young Kamilaroi woman has attracted over 100,000 signatures with her online campaign. She, and many others reckon that we should all be proud of 60,000 odd years of indigenous history and flying the flag alongside the national and NSW state flags would be an appropriate expression of that pride. Personally, I'd love to see the red, yellow and black flag more often.

It doesn't take long to eat up some miles on the Newcastle Freeway, followed by the fast Pacific Highway where I sing Frank Sinatra songs (*Moon River* being my best performance) at the top of my lungs, as my single-cylinder engine drones on. My venerable Kawasaki 649cc motorcycle, like me is old-school and not very complex. Since its introduction in 1987 it's basically remained unchanged, again, just like me ("yeah, right!" I can hear my wife laugh!) There are plenty of things that it's not. It's not the fastest away from the lights or the prettiest. It's not the most expensive and probably not the most comfortable. What it *is*, is robust, and unpretentious, lacking the modern gizmos, like traction control, adjustable riding modes, ABS brakes, and fuel injection to name the most basic things that manufacturers seem to think everyone wants. Its massive fuel tank means that it won't splutter to a halt before the next roadhouse or town. And with its 21inch front wheel, high ground clearance and

bash plate, it's designed to handle rough roads when the tarmac ends, as I feel sure it will, at some stage on my journey. Legendary for its rugged versatility, the big single has a functional beauty that many motorcyclists fail to appreciate. As one advertisement put it, the KLR is, "Not good at anything but good at everything."

At Kempsey's Information Centre a helpful volunteer directs me further up the road to the arty little town of Bellingen in the growing dusk. I find the YHA Hostel and grab the last bunk in a four-man dorm, praying there are no snorers, as I'm a light sleeper and they have been the bane of my travelling life. As I book in, I produce my gold YHA life membership card with a flourish. "That's worthless now mate," the warden says dismissively, "you automatically get membership these days when you book a bed."

It's Trivia Night at the Federal Hotel and they're doing a brisk trade as I settle the dust with a pint of Coopers. Before leaving in the chilly morning I chat with an English travel-guide writer and his Australian, yoga-instructor wife as they eat their muesli. Their cute seven-year-old son wants to teach me origami, but I insist I'm not patient enough. The father is reading about Donald Trump's meeting with Putin in Helsinki on his phone. "Says here," he laughs, "that Trump, 'projecting nothing but weakness, rolled over and invited Putin to tickle him.'"

It's cold leaving Bellengin and I switch my heated handlebar grips on. "Pussy" I can hear you say but I regard it as a Health and Safety issue. The Pacific Highway is more interesting now as it takes me through towns, rather than passing them by. At Coffs Harbour I ride down to the jetty to see the fishing boats and watch a pelican glide across the water, its pouch full of fish.

As I travel up the coast towards Queensland, a record dry spell is causing eastern Australia's worst drought in a century. In parts of inland New South Wales, livestock are starving, as a dry winter and high temperatures have severely depleted grazing. Australia is not alone. Wildfires are ravaging Greece and even Sweden has asked for international assistance to help tackle an epidemic of wild fires. And to think, there are still Climate Change sceptics!

Past the Yuraygir National Park, largest coastal park in the state and through the Bom Bom State Forest, the air is thick with a blue smoky haze from recent bush fires. Just past Grafton in the tiny town of Ulmarra it's time for another coffee, this one not so good – too weak and only luke warm. I drink it nonetheless at a picnic table on the banks of the wide and tranquil River Clarence. "This used to be a famous river port town," an old timer with a huge nicotine-stained, white beard tells me when he sees me writing. His fox terrier pisses up my table leg as if to emphasise he master's words.

Just outside Brisbane I plug in my GPS and punch in my mate Foz's address. Over my engine noise and traffic, I struggle to follow the well-modulated tones of the woman giving me directions. It's still an ordeal, jousting with manic rush-hour traffic intent on getting back to hearth and home, but it would have been a very frustrating exercise without it. Foz (aka Paul Fozzard) went to University with my wife in London back in the 80's and like many friends, we haven't seen as much of him recently as we'd have liked. It's great to catch up with him, his Kiwi wife Sharon and three boisterous school-age boys, one of whom has vacated his bedroom for me.

Tales and Trails Down Under

Shortly after moving to Sydney in 1989, Foz came and stayed with us in Erskineville and we reminisce on some hilarious times. I was laying bricks for a company in the eastern suburbs and got Foz a start as a brickie's labourer on the same site. It was boom time and I remember the look of amazement on Foz's face when he opened his first wage packet. "I think they've overpaid me George" he said!

Sad as it is to leave the Fozard's, I'm soon back in my 'happy place', in Percy's saddle, accelerating up the Bruce Highway on a sunny morning, despite the heavy traffic and blustery wind doing its best to bring my mood down. I'm briefly tempted to turn right and visit Noosa Heads, a spot I'd first visited and had a great time camping at in 1980 but know full well it will lead to disappointment as today it's full of high-rises, expensive boutiques and fancy restaurants where tourists sip their over-priced chardonnay and flaunt their wealth. Chip on my shoulder? Who, me?

After riding around Gympie in a vain attempt to find a coffee shop I finally fetch up at a café in tiny Tiaro which is doing a roaring trade. I'm enjoying my coffee, eating my egg sandwich and reading my James Burke novel at a table to myself, when an elderly couple arrive looking for a seat. "You can sit here," I offer. They turn out to be real characters with a hint of mischief in their eyes. "Norman Wurst," the man introduces himself, "and I'm a proper sausage!" His wife Joy is obviously used to this routine. "This gentleman said I could sit on his lap dear," he says to her and winks at me. They both smile and settle in their seats. As they eat their barramundi and chips, they tell me their story.

Now retired and in his late 80's, Norman spent four years in Alice Springs and seven in Papunya in the Northern Territory, teaching Aboriginals how to be pastors on behalf of the Lutheran Church. "You could say they got the best of the Wurst," says Norman and winks again. "Papunya is an Aboriginal community about 240 kilometres west of Alice. Literally in the middle of nowhere," offers Joy, "they're mainly Luritja and Pintupi people who live there."

While Norman was spreading the word, Joy worked in the thriving art scene in Papunya. "I worked at the Papunya Tjupi Aboriginal

Arts organisation where about 100 local artists paint," she tells me. "Have you heard of Doris Bush Nungarrayi?" she asks. I shake my head. "How about Albert Namatjira?" asks Norman with a mouthful of chips. I nod, (yes, I've heard of him). "Well he painted there in the early days." They tell me that they'll never retire and currently live in Toowoomba where they do volunteer work, helping refugees from Sudan, Congo and Burundi to acclimatise to the Australian way of life.

The last 50 kilometres of the day before I lock Percy up behind the Bundaberg Grand Hotel and book in, provide some great riding. And a couple of quiet beers (Queenslanders couldn't give a XXXX for any other beer) at the almost empty Club Hotel followed by a stroll along the river ends my day.

In the morning I get an email from my brother Malcolm in London, who asks, if I ever get lonely on these long rides? I take the smaller roads heading north towards Rockhampton where I plan to leave the coast and head inland. As I ride, I think about my brother's question. And I realise that for someone used to and comfortable in their own company, solitude becomes something of a drug – a thing to cherish. So, the answer Malcolm, is "no."

Through vast stands of sugar cane, the small towns of Rosedale and Lowmead, the Mount Colosseum National Park and past my first dead kangaroo, a big grey, I emerge onto the Bruce Highway for coffee at the Big Crab Café in Miriam Vale. At a road works red light I see my first live 'roos, half a dozen or so of them grazing on a hillside in the distance.

I stop for lunch in Rockhampton, parking my bike on the footpath where I can sit alongside. An Aboriginal family, mum and three kids wander by. The eldest boy, wearing a rugby jersey and a cheeky grin says, "Nice bike mister," before skateboarding off.

A4	CAPRICORN HIGHWAY
Westwood	35
Emerald	254
Barcaldine	562
Longreach	669

Chapter Three.

INTO THE OUTBACK

*"Into the great wide open
Under them skies of blue"*

Tom Petty and the Heartbreakers.

It gives me a little thrill to leave the populated east coast, for this afternoon I'm heading into the outback. I'm not sure where the 'outback' starts but this certainly looks like it and each revolution of Percy's wheels takes me deeper into it. The Capricorn Highway stretches on ahead, disappearing into the distance, spinifex and saltbush on either side while the winter sunshine dances on the tarmac. The land is as flat as a pancake, as though it's been levelled by a giant steam roller. Is it warmer already or is it just me? I feel a bit guilty for not riding up to Cairns before heading west but I've arranged a couple of interviews in Longreach and don't want to be late.

The Highway runs alongside a major rail link which carries enormous coal trains from Central Queensland to Gladstone and other east coast ports. Along with the black stuff, this is also cattle country and signs warn of unfenced areas.

My body is getting acclimatised to riding now. My highway pegs are a godsend, enabling me to move my butt around in the saddle as

I stretch my legs in various positions. I felt a bit of a twat with them back home in Christchurch but out here they are very fitting. I can also lift one foot (or both) and rest them on the top of my engine crash bars. High above me an eagle hawk wheels, probably looking for fresh road kill.

I'm now in the Bowen Basin which is home to several large coal mines of which the modern little town of Blackwater, 'Coal Capital of Queensland' is the service centre. Some 15 million tons are transported to Gladstone annually. With 500 kilometres on the clock I decide to call it a day and end up in a well-appointed cabin, surrounded by high-viz-clad miners.

You won't be surprised to learn that Blackwater, discovered by Ludwig Leichardt in 1845, is so named because of the dark water in nearby creeks believed to have been caused by coal deposits, Its population has halved from a high of 10,000 in the mid 1970's.

Back on the road, after an "oh shit" moment when Percy refused to start, I'm contemplating my naval, figuratively speaking, brooding on the relativity of time and wondering how far my tank of fuel will last in this headwind, when I swerve around a dead 'roo and a whistling kite launches itself in my direction, twisting away at the last second. I sometimes get a bit of a warning of road kill ahead by the smell of meat putrefying in the sun.

The light out here has an intensity that gives the most mundane things a startling clarity. I wish I was a painter and could whip out my easel and water colours, to capture it but make do with another digital photo. The landscape looks a lot like Texas, minus the nodding oil derricks.

When I first came to this magnificent country a lifetime ago on a working holiday visa in 1980, full of Vim and invincible, I clearly remember my first trip into the bush. How, used to the watery sunlight of England, I found the red dirt, brilliant sunlight and gum trees as alien a landscape as I'd seen in my young life.

As my bike eats up the miles, I pass the occasional dirt road and mail box indicating some kind of human presence. Emerald is buzzing with well-turned-out travellers (I'm guessing they must be the owners of all the white 4-wheel-drives towing caravans and campervans I've been sharing the road with) and an Italian-themed coffee shop seems a million miles away from the awesome emptiness that lurks on the edge of town.

About 200 kilometers from Longreach I cross the Great Dividing Range at 444 metres. I'm now in the Lake Aire Basin and if there was

any water around, it would flow westward with me. I'm suddenly amongst a forest of smallish red ant hills that extend away from the road as far as I can see.

In a run-down pub in Jericho I forsake my usual coffee for a cold beer – it would probably have been instant anyway. I ask the portly owner how long it should take me to get to Darwin. "I could do it in three days," he replies. "But on your bike, youz should piss it in a week. Youz going right round, are yuz?"

I nod as he hands me my beer in a stubby holder, "On ya mate!" he says, before serving the only other customer.

Road trains thunder past heading east, hauling cattle to ships, abattoirs or greener pastures as I carry on to Longreach, which emerges in the late afternoon. On the way I pass two emus on the road side of a stock fence behind some stunted trees. One swivels its head as I ride past, a brief vignette in my peripheral vision.

Friend of a friend Lisa kindly puts me up at the Pastoral College where she works and has arranged for me to chat with a couple of colourful locals. She's a great lady and incredibly helpful. I've barely unloaded the bike before John arrives, looking like he's just stepped out of a Western movie. After a firm handshake I hop into his ute and we're off in a cloud of dust to his place of work.

Rural Trainer
John Arnold

As we drive, we get to know each other. John still has his wide-brimmed hat on and with his boots, jeans and steely gaze, he looks every inch the cowboy. He's a tall and rangy 62, but looks younger. He was born in the outback, in a little town on the Queensland/NSW border where his father managed sheep and cattle properties. It's the only life he's ever known, and his earliest memories are of being a tiny boy, following old stockmen around, riding a worn-out old stock horse.

"I came here when I was two, so I've been around Longreach pretty much most of my life; I guess that make me a local," he says laconically.

John has been a stockman himself but says his preferred work over the years has been as a contract horse breaker, moving from property to property, breaking horses in for the stockmen to ride, a job he's been doing since he was 21. "You must have known your stuff at such a young age," I say.

"Oh yeah ..." he replies, "I guess I had some good teachers. But

back then the horsemanship was kinda rough and ready. There wasn't much science in what we did compared to today. In the last 20 years there's been so much knowledge imported into Australia, some from America, some from Europe."

John reckons the standard of horsemanship has improved markedly over the years. "The old Australian stockman was a good man with a rough horse, but today the horses are purpose-bred for the job." We pull up by a huge corral where a small herd stand around swishing their tails and snorting. These are John's personal horses which he fed earlier. I ask an obvious question, "so you must love horses John?"

"Yeah ... you've gotta love horses. If you can turn what you love into your living, you're laughing aren't you? But they're all different personalities. Good and bad ones. The American quarter-horse was brought over in the 1950s and a lot of cross-breeding went on with them – plus we still have the typical Australian stock horse which is a thoroughbred horse. You've got to be open-minded. The only horse I'm looking for today George, is a better one than I rode yesterday."

He suggests we drive over to the Pastoral College facilities where he spends most of his working day. "Normally there'd be 50 or 60 horses waiting in the paddocks out there, hanging around waiting for us to work with them," says John as we wander around the steel fenced corrals and buildings that make up the facility that is owned and funded by the State Government and managed by the Queensland Agricultural Training Colleges Corporation.

"Basically," explains John, "we have young people coming here who are looking to work on a property. We don't teach them management, we teach them the basic things like stock handling, horse riding, branding, fencing and vehicle maintenance. The sort of skills needed to work on a property."

It's quiet at the moment because the students have just been sent to their work placements. Some are placed on properties with as many as 50,000 head of cattle, working with staff getting practical experience in the industry. Students can start here as young as 16, with six and 12-month courses available, with a qualification at the end that is recognised nationwide.

"About 15 or 20 years ago the Government made up a syllabus called the National Training Packages, which meant that if you did a subject in the Northern Territory, it'd be the same as what they taught you in Tasmania," he says in the soft, measured tone that

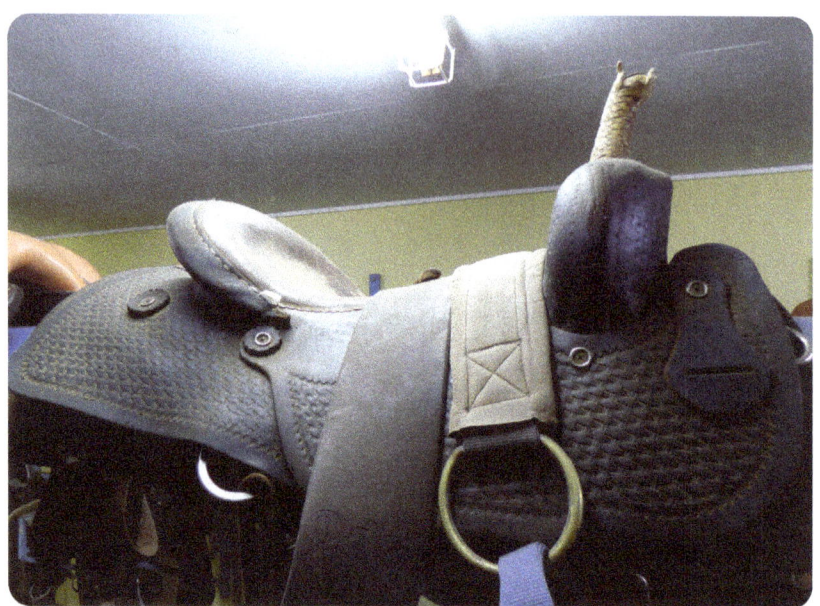

I imagine has calmed many a nervous student over the years. We enter the tack room which has that unmistakable smell of well-looked-after leather.

He slaps a beautiful saddle, one of many sitting in a row on brackets, "This is your typical Australian saddle that we've used here for the past two hundred years. It was derived from the old English hunting saddle but because our horses are a bit wilder and we do some crazy things with them, we've put these knee pads in and also made the back a bit higher than the hunting saddle. Over the past 50 years of so we've also added some American features so this is called a half-breed saddle, half American and half Australian."

A typical saddle here is worth around $5,000 which surprises me as there must be so much leather around. "Well, believe it or not leather is ridiculously expensive. With the millions of cattle that are slaughtered in Australia," John says, "there are only two tanneries left here. The leather for most of these saddles would probably have been imported from America."

John has been training jillaroos and jackaroos here for 32 years, but he gives the impression that he's still as passionate as when he started out.

"It must give you a lot of satisfaction when you send a young person out, knowing that you've done a good job," I venture.

"Yeah … when you see them go out and do a good job, it does give you a lot of satisfaction," he ponders for a second, "A lot of young people these days are content to be Joe-averages so when I hear back that a young person from here has been a success, it's good. I wouldn't want to take all the credit, of course, but it's nice to know that you may have fostered that desire to learn and improve."

Some students become contract musterers, some use their new skills to go back to the family property, some become professional horse trainers and some use the qualifications as a stepping stone for vetinary college or University. "I've had students become anything from farriers and chiropractors to helicopter pilots; you name it," says John, "the horse industry is pretty diverse, they could end up anywhere."

I wonder aloud if young people today are that interested in getting their hands dirty and whether there will be enough people to fill the places at the college. "No George, Australia has a chronic shortage of rural workers and in January and February my phone rings off the hook with property owners looking for young people."

I ask John if he's ever been injured at work. "Touch wood, I've had a remarkably injury-free career considering," he replies. "I broke a couple of ribs this year for the first time but there was no malice involved. The little horse just pulled its leg away as the flies were pretty bad and she accidentally bumped me in the ribs. But I've always tried to ride quality horses, use quality gear and follow sound equine handling philosophies and guidelines. A few people out there are getting broken bone,s but sometimes accidents just happen."

With the growing trend towards people trying to eat less meat, I ask John how he sees the future of the cattle industry. "Well there's such a shortage of protein world-wide," comes the immediate response, "and with the growing world population, we've got to feed people. So as long as there's one cow left in Australia, we're going to need someone to muster it. You can have all the drones and technology in the world but you'll still need workers."

The Longreach area and western Queensland has experienced

years of ongoing drought with summer rains failing for the past eight. I ask John how climate change has influenced the cattle industry. "Yeah … it's become something that people have to work with," he says. "Management and grazing strategies have had to change severely to work with the climate. But there was certainly no global warming this morning. It was only one degree!"

John tells me that there is no gender bias in the industry these days and there are just as many young women as men in his classes. In the last 20 years there's been a huge increase in the number of females working in the rural industry. "Girls certainly can do it," says John, "I even know of female head stockmen, which would have been unheard of 40 years ago."

"Shouldn't that be 'stockperson' John?" I ask tongue-in-cheek and we laugh.

Finally, I ask him how much longer he can see himself doing this. "Well," he considers, "while I can beat those young fellas to the breakfast table and shoe more horses in a day, then I'll carry on doing it." Another thoughtful pause, "I don't think I'm past my used-by-date just yet."

Morning finds me roaming the streets, along with a throng of other tourists. The café on the main street has wi-fi and serves up a fair eggs, bacon and coffee – not a bad way to start the day. I love coffee shops, consider myself something of a connoisseur of them, in fact. I feel as comfortable ensconced in one, coffee, book or notebook and pen in front of me, as I do in my own living room. At times it can feel almost voyeuristic, this sharing of space with complete strangers. I love the unspoken contract between patrons – we're sharing this space, sharing a few moments in time, yet we're apart. A smile, a nod of recognition, an exchange of pleasantries, a statement of togetherness. A brief respite in a journey from A to B, or indeed one's life.

The street is bathed in brilliant sunshine as a flock of pink galahs (also known as pink or grey cockatoos) hurtle by at head-height.

After trying on every Akubra in the hat shop, I ride to the Australian Stockman's Hall of Fame and wander the 2,500 square metres of floor space. Hugh Sawrey, ex-stockman and renowned artist, founded the museum which was opened by the Queen in 1988. Many displays tell the stories of Aboriginals, European explorers, settlers and the unsung heroes of Outback Australia.

Just down the road is another tourist attraction, The Qantas Founders Outback Museum. In the car park are three dusty KLR 650s with "Burke and Wills 2018 Tour" stickers on their screens. I keep a weather-eye open for the riders but don't see them. Two museums in one day is pushing it for me. After half an hour I'm usually getting a bit panicky and looking for the exit, but this one is different, and I manage almost 45 minutes! I discover that Qantas is an acronym for Queensland and Northern Territory Aerial Services, and that it's the 3rd oldest airline in the world. Its original headquarters was up the highway in Winton before it re-located to Longreach in 1921.

It's nice to have a cruisy day and I catch up on some writing and even manage a nana nap. My host Lisa is an absolute gem and has arranged for me to interview the editor of the local rag. It's very informal – I'm to meet him tonight at the bar in the RSL.

I'm somewhat spoilt having been brought up on English pub

culture, and certainly do miss it but it must be said that for people travelling through, like myself, the RSLs hit the spot. Like a lot of institutions in the 21st century, they are having trouble staying relevant with the younger generation, and many RSLs have amalgamated with other clubs in an effort to survive. The 'No Smoking' policy hit them really hard according to the barmaid, who is wearing a tight T shirt telling me that Elvis didn't in fact die in 1977 but still lives! As I've been staring at her chest for the past five seconds, I feel a comment is required. "Nice T-shirt," is all I can muster but she smiles without eye contact.

Newspaper Editor
Colin Jackson

Colin and I sit at the bar, a couple of schooners in front of us, VB for him, light beer for me as I'm on my bike. The convivial hubbub of conversation, laughter and clinking glasses fills the air. Colin's just finished work and walked from the office which is only ten minutes away. He's not impressed with my dictaphone. "My grandfather and father taught me not to use tape. I just took notes and stored it all up here," he says, tapping his head.

Colin is the editor of the *Longreach Leader*, a position he's had for about a year. He's proud to say that he's the 3rd generation of a North Queensland newspaper family. "This paper in Longreach started in January 1923 and my family's paper, the *Home Hill Observer* started a month later in February 1923."

Home Hill, he explains is just south of Townsville and was named, like other towns in the region after places made famous in the Crimean War of 1853-56. Apparently, the sign writer decided to drop the 'l' from Holme Hill and it was never changed.

Colin and his brother sold the family paper when he was 40,

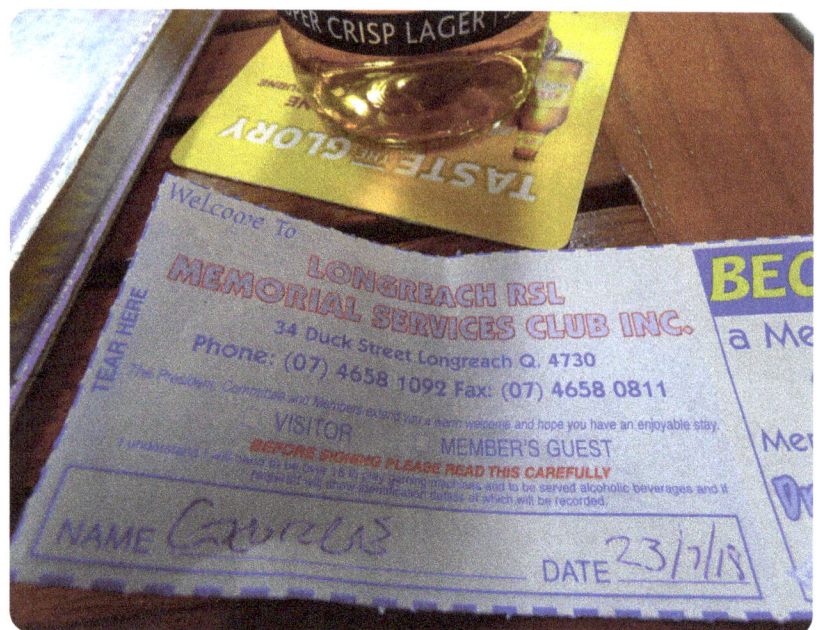

his brother staying on as editor and Colin joining the MTAQ (Motor Trades Association of Queensland) where he worked for the next ten years and started up four new magazines. "When you see opportunity you run with it," he says. "I started a tyre magazine which took me all over the world. The highlight was visiting South Korea and the Hankook tyre factory. The Koreans were just so proud of their work."

Colin also visited the border and the demilitarised zone. And reckons the North Koreans could invade and take over any time they chose. "It's a good job the Yanks are there," he says, "and I like the old Trumpster. He's a no-nonsense bloke. Don't get in my way or I'll kick your arse! That's how you do it. Keep them guessing."

After being laid-off, Colin, a graphic artist by trade went out on his own. "I can operate printing presses and I did my journalism cadetship under my father and did work for many magazines, so I was a jack-of-all-trades," he says and sips his beer appreciatively.

He lived in Brisbane for a while but prefers the country life. "Whether it was the Home Hill era of years ago or Longreach today," says Colin without preamble, "you just can't get people out of the cities, I don't know why. Why would people want to cram themselves into a city when they could have the wide-open spaces, I'll never bloody know. I know we're 13 hours from Brisbane and eight hours from Rockhampton and we're remote, but I just love it out here. The friendliness of Longreach is incredible."

I ask him how he ended up here. "Well my father pulled me out of school at 13, so I've been working for 58 years. In July last year I thought I'd retire but I soon got incredibly bored. All I was doing was putting my suit on and going out for lunch with my old Army mates. Then a mate phoned me up and asked if I'd like to come to Longreach, all-expenses-paid for a couple of weeks." He takes another pull on his beer and wipes the froth off his top lip. "I came here originally as a reliever, as the editor was on sick leave."

I get more beers in and Colin digresses. "What about those grey nomads. Some of them are shocking drivers! I saw one pull out of a camp site just down the highway without looking and a Landcruiser drove straight through the caravan which of course wasn't insured."

"Was that a story in your paper?" I ask. "No, I missed that one. Trouble is out here you hear about these things too late. I've got such a vast area to cover." The bar manager wanders by and Colin collars him, "is it stew tonight or are you still calling it a 'roast'?" he wants to know. The bar manager smiles, accustomed to the ribbing.

I get Colin back on topic. "So, I wrote for lots of magazines after I left the MTAQ. With the *Blues* and *Outback* magazines people would ring me and say, you've got to come to our festival, and I'd be expected to go to every one. Out here, the one to go to is in Winton Outback Festival, it's a ripper. It's just a typical festival where people come together and have a great time. So, I often visited this area and I grew to love it." Another mate wanders in and exchanges a few words with him. It's obvious Colin is well liked at his local.

"I can park anywhere," he continues, "I walk down here in ten minutes and have two or three beers. I can come in here, people know where I sit, they come and talk to me and I find out what I need to know. I hear some things I can't print and some things I can save up."

Colin loves books and is still waiting for his library to arrive from Brisbane, which he had left in a hurry last year. He's an author in his own right, having penned, *A Centenary of Road Transport in Australia – 1900 to 2010*, and a book he says he enjoyed writing immensely, *The Life and Times of The Nullarbor Kid*.

"I laughed the whole time, writing that because I could relate to the stories. This old truckie (the Nullarbor Kid) used to drive between Perth and Sydney way back when it was just a track," he says. "He wore a side-arm, a Colt .45 too. Nothing small, something that's going to stop you. He got stuck in the middle of nowhere for three months once. He had to wait for another truck coming through to take a part to Sydney, and then wait for one going west to drop the new part off."

I'd forgotten about the custom in Australian RSLs of playing the *Last Post* every night. We all stand in silence for a couple of minutes as the TV screens flash images of war zones. 'At the going down of the sun, and in the morning, we will remember. Lest we forget,' a voice intones as the bugle trumpets. The screen nearest to us has stubbornly continued playing a rock video and Colin isn't impressed. "This is when you need a Colt .45," he says to the barmaid, "to shoot that screen out."

I steer him back on to the *Longreach Leader*. Colin reckons the paper was on its last legs when he took over but he just applied proper newspaper principles to it and he thinks it's recovering. He regards himself as a servant of the locals, saying, "I was having coffee with the State Premier recently and I told her, 'I'm a representative of the people too.' So many people have shown me things and befriended me, I just feel I need to give back."

He says that he took up his new post, the paper was at such a low ebb, he doubts if it would have survived the financial year. "When I arrived, I said to the staff of five women, 'these are your parameters, and this is the job I'd like you to do.' But they're all good and I love them. They just wanted a bit of direction. So, I've been giving them a bit of training and it's just overwhelming how well they're doing."

He's not a big fan of political correctness, preferring to 'say it like it is.' He thinks that a country paper can get away with things that a city paper couldn't. "Nobody's going to complain out here!" he says.

Colin tries to work with the Outback Tourism Association as much as possible. "Wherever they go, we'll give them 500 papers, say 100 of the last five issues and they'll put a heap on every bar in places like Windorah and Birdsville, where there are no newsagents." All they ask is a gold coin donation in the tin for the Royal Flying Doctor Service for each newspaper.

"Because they're worshipped out here George," he says, "you may have seen the designated strips of highway for them to land on," and I nod, then ask him if he plans to stay in Longreach.

"Look, I love the place I'm from, Home Hill, but I also love this place. It's full of characters. Genuine, generous people. So, I don't think I'll ever leave. I'd love to have someone of around 45 or 50 to take over and bring the paper forward. So, my message is, if you want to do something with a sense of achievement, if you're sociable and want to get to know the people, then come out here and you'll have a ball!"

Out of Longreach the land is as flat as still water – open ranchland, punctuated with stands of bush and scrub. Large sections of highway, which is now named Matilda, are un-fenced, so my wildlife radar is on high alert. Cattle stations are ridiculously huge. The largest in Queensland is Davenport Downs which is over 15,000 square kilometres or 3,730,000 acres in size – about the same size as East Timor.

If approaching Longreach was like Texas then this stretch reminds me of Botswana or Namibia, minus of course, colourful Africans, zebra and antelope. Every 50ks or so there is a rest area, with shaded picnic table and toilets. I sit at one after a while and finish reading *Heaven's Prisoners*, once again in awe of James Lee Burkes writing. Sometimes it seems that reading these days is a guilty pleasure, a bit like smoking. I still get the odd speculative glance when people see me reading in a coffee shop or pub on my own. Maybe it's becoming a counter-culture? It's always been a very private act for me. A chance to disappear for an hour into another world. Reading a novel often confirms that implicit in us all is a universe of possibilities. There's no feeling like immersing yourself in the comfortable cotton wool of your favourite author's world.

I'm in no hurry, as I only plan to ride 200ks today. With a sigh I close my book and leave the muggy, wet bayou country of Louisiana. I clunk the Kawasaki into gear, let out the clutch and enter the dry outback again. Kilometre after kilometre. The outback, an entity all to itself, seemingly indifferent to the world's goings-on. A huge road train towing four trailers buffets me, sucking hot air along with it as it heads east.

The long economic boom in Australia has seen a sharp increase in freight traffic and a subsequent increase in accidents involving heavy goods vehicles. Since the last recession way back in 1991 (and I remember it well as we'd recently signed on the dotted, for our first mortgage, with a 17.25% interest rate!) road freight has increased 150%. Today a staggering 2.5 billion tonnes of freight is carried on the roads each year.

I read in the paper recently that NSW Roads Minister is consider-

ing cunning plans to help truckers concentrate on the route ahead. One idea is to install a camera that monitors driver's eyelids and how many times they look away from the road. If they are deemed to be tardy in this regard, an alarm will sound, and the seat will vibrate. A more extreme idea is to administer an electric shock via a bracelet if the driver looks away from the windscreen for more than two seconds. I'd be interested to see how these ideas are received by truckers!

I cruise around Winton's wide sunny streets looking for coffee, finally parking in the main drag and wandering over to a young guy who's climbing onto his Suzuki DR 650, a bike similar to mine. He's a fellow cross-country man by the look of his gear. It's plain that he sees me heading over for a chat but just pulls away, eyes front. Ah, well, it takes all sorts I suppose. The pretty young girl who makes my coffee is from Exeter in Devon and says she can't understand people who want to live in cities. I sip my flat white, swat flies, listen to Stevie Wonder on the radio, and stare out at the almost-empty main street, expecting a tumbleweed or two to blow down it.

The North Gregory Hotel in Winton is where Banjo Patterson performed Australia's unofficial national anthem *Waltzing Matilda* for the first time in 1895. Winton is also the centre for dinosaur country, as thousands of huge fossilised footprints are to be found in the nearby Lark Quarry Conservation Park. Tourists are reminded of this by plastic rubbish bins on the pavement made in the shape of dinosaur feet.

    I phone Mick, who's kindly offered talk to me and put me up on his nearby cattle station, and ask him for directions. He's busy mustering but tells me to come up anyway and make myself at home. The ride out to Windermere Station is marvelous. A couple of kms out of town I turn on to a red dirt road and soon find myself riding across a huge dusty plain following tyre tracks towards a collection of buildings in the distance. Mick's wife Anne, is expecting me and I'm soon dumping my gear in the cosy spare room. The farmhouse is built on tall piles to allow for the regular floods, allowing Mick to build his own bar under the house. It's here that I now find myself, beer-in-hand with Anne and Mick's off-sider Dan. Mick plays barman. He asks me what I'd like and when I say, "VB please," they all laugh and hi-five each other. "At last we can get rid of that shit!" he says, Queensland XXXX drinker to the core. Percy is parked in the bar next to us.

Cattleman
Mick Seymour

I place my dictaphone on the bar and tell Mick, tanned, blue eyed, and as solid as a bull, not to be intimidated by it. "The last time I had one of them pointed at me, it was a policeman," he says, and I realise that Mick wouldn't be intimidated by much at all. I start by asking if he's always been 'on the land.'

"Most of the time," he replies, "although I wasn't born on the land. I was born in Cloncurry – my father was a shearer, a slaughterman and a butcher." He sips his XXXX and puts my can of VB into a 'Pub in the Bush' tinny-holder. His hands are big, and work-worn. "You haven't moved far then," I say.

"Well I *have* – I've just gone in a big circle."

"Well tell me of your journey," I say in my most corny interviewer voice, half Parkinson, half Oprah, which makes everyone smile.

"I left school at 15 and took off on my own, working on cattle stations all over Queensland. I worked for Stanbroke, a big cattle company for over a decade." Another sip of beer. "I wasn't much good at school. I wasn't stupid, I just didn't like school work. I hated homework, so I'd get this girl I knew, to do it for me."

It was while contract mustering around Clairmont in the Central Highlands that Mick met Anne. The couple, in their early twenties were soon married and had purchased their own property, a little 5,000-acre place near Clairmont. "We also looked after the property next door which belonged to a Doctor, which we bought off him," Mick says

They then purchased Riversleigh Station in the Gulf of Carpentaria, which was around a million acres in size. I once again marvel at the sheer scale of properties in Australia. "At the time," Mick says, "the station was undergoing a clean-up programme – TB eradication, feral cattle, etc – so was a good buy. But interest rates were 20% and it was tough going."

Mick and Anne then fought a legal battle with the Government that would result in 200,000 acres of the property becoming part of the Boodjamulla (Lawn Hill) National Park and a World Heritage Site, containing fossil deposits that tell the evolutionary history of some of the most distinctive and isolated mammals in the world, dating back 25 million years.

Mike isn't very forthcoming on the details, saying simply that it's 'a long story' and I don't press him. "I think we were the first station to have land forcibly taken from us. But the Governor General signed the papers and that was that. The compensation was a piddle-up-a-post. Like I say, it's a long story and hurtful one," he dismisses it with an, "anyway it was a good fight. Then the lead and the zinc mines came up there and the Aboriginals moved in. They were never that interested when we were just mustering cows, of course," he says with pursed-lips and a shrug.

Then in 1996 they sold up and purchased the 165,000-acre Split Rock Station, 160 kilometres to the south. "It was largely undeveloped, so for the next eight or nine years we went contract mustering and droving to supplement the place."

Mick and Anne would take all their horses, trucks, camping gear and seven or eight employees to go muster other people's cattle for a daily fee, he explains.

"We'd go up into the Gulf, to places like Cliffdale, Beesbrook and Escott. Some pretty wild places, but it was exciting. We'd round them up, move them to the yard, brand 'em, do pregnancy testing and weening – all the normal things. So, after all the expenses there was a bit of cream and this paid to develop Split Rock."

"And three kids at boarding school," adds Anne. I ask Mick how many people it takes to run a property of that size. "Not many," he says, "you just have to work harder, day and night when you're still young," he says and hands me another VB.

Then, when one of their sons decided he wanted to become a butcher, Mick and Anne bought the butcher shop in the town of Camooweal, not far from Split Rock Station and while they were at it, bought two more in Mt Isa. Mick would slaughter his own cattle at Camooweal and take them to Mt Isa for sale.

"So, you're a bit of an entrepreneur then?"

"Well," replies Mick, nodding in acknowledgement, "we did that for about ten years, and meanwhile had bought another two properties at Tambo."

With Anne now living and working in Mt Isa as a councillor, and Mick constantly travelling between Split Rock and Tambo, they decided to a buy property half-way between, which is how they ended up near Winton at Windamere Station. "It's an ideal situation.

If we're trucking cattle from Split Rock, where we breed, to Tambo, we can give 'em a blow for a couple of months here. So, there it is George, that's our life," says Mick as he opens another can of XXXX for him and his mate Dan who hasn't taken off his battered akubra and has been silent so far.

Mick and Anne have been married almost 40 years and have three sons. One works in the mines at Mt Isa, one is an electrician in Cairns, while the other one, William, runs Split Rock Station, while not working as a contract chopper pilot. "They're all good boys," says Mick.

Dan suggests that I visit Will at Split Rock as he's not 'far off the track' and he's more articulate than his father, and Mick readily agrees.

I get onto the topical subject of the lack of rain. "You used to be able to rely on it," says Dan.

"The first storms would come in November along with the Melbourne Cup," offers Mick, "you'd either be fighting fires or rained in – But not anymore. It's like sex mate – you never know when you're gonna get it," another sip of beer, "but I've never had a bad bit of rain yet!"

"Do you put that down to global warming?" I ask, knowing from an earlier chat that he's a bit of a sceptic.

"No – put that down to Julia Gillard and Kevin Rudd being Prime Ministers!"

"Seriously though," says Anne, "since about 2000 the weather's gone crazy. Nobody gets flooded out anymore. We used to spend weeks on a station because we couldn't get out."

"I remember," adds Mick, "at Riversleigh we lived between two big rivers and it rained so much one year, we couldn't get out for four months. The big wet just doesn't come any more."

I then ask him the same thing I asked 'John Arnold' back in Longreach. "Have you had many injuries?" and get a similar answer.

"No, not really. You get more these days through lack of experience. It's all about CS George. Common fuckin' sense!"

When I talk about the future of life on the land in Australia, Mick

suggests that I should probably talk to Anne if I want an intellectual viewpoint. "I just believe," says Anne, who joins us at the bar, "that if things carry on the way they have these last few years, I can't imagine all the cattle properties remaining sustainable. I think we're going to have lots of people moving off the land. Hopefully they'll move into the smaller towns where they'd be most welcome, but they'll probably go to the cities."

"That's what the Government want," says Mick, who I suspect is something of a conspiracy theorist. "Last year 30 people moved out of Winton. Where properties used to have a dozen or so people living on them, now there's just a mother and father."

"Take this house, George. It was built by the Mitchells and they had 12 kids," says Anne.

"That's coz she said, 'yes' more often," jokes Mick.

Mick still enjoys his work, though at 62 he says he's isn't a fan of yard work, as he's not as mobile as he once was. And with technology he feels the fun has gone out of it. "It may have been harder years ago but there was a certain camaraderie. You'd work with a bunch of good blokes and camp out in your swags and stay with the cattle. You didn't come home to wi-fi and the internet. Some people who come out to work in the bush don't want to start at the bottom.

But they won't progress unless they do it hard and there's no easy way with cattle."

Mick reckons he tolerates a lot more that he would have 30 years ago. I suggest that perhaps he's mellowed a bit. "I've just learned to compromise I think," he says.

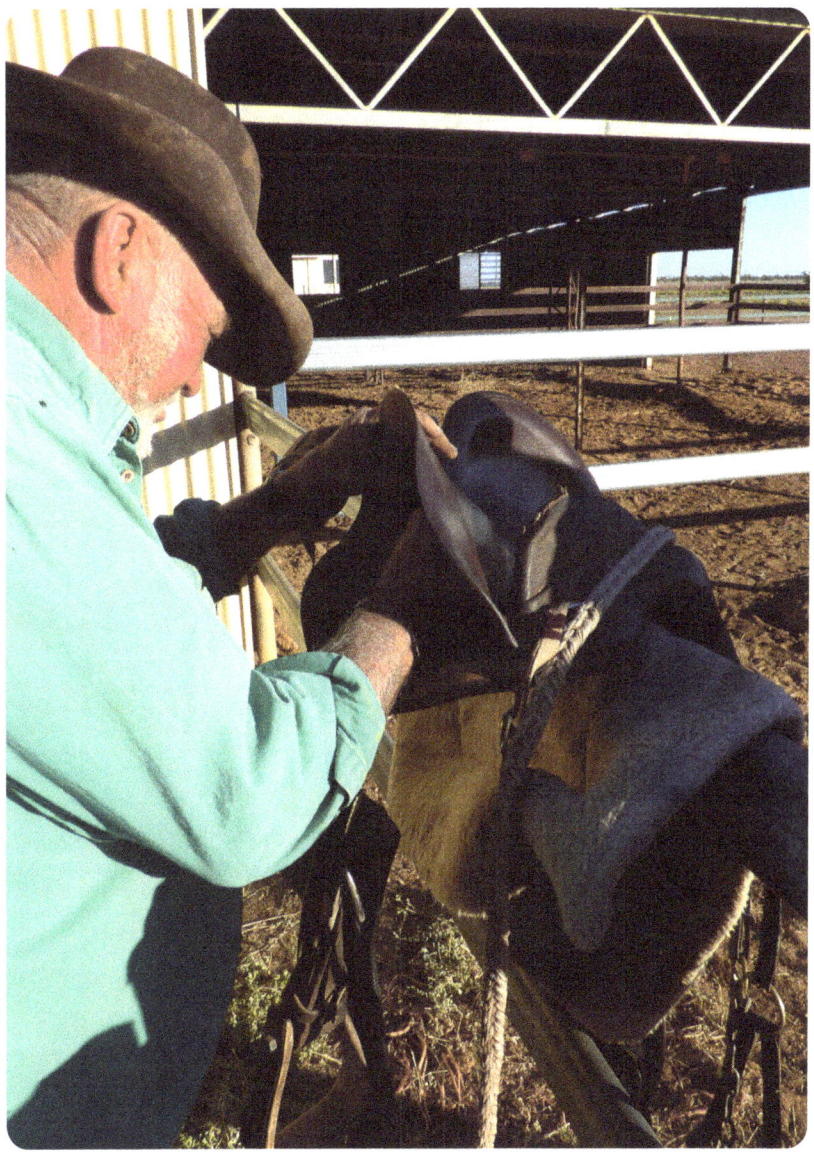

Chapter Four.

THE NEVER NEVER

*"And as we ride on down the road.
Our shadows taller than our souls."*

Led Zeppelin.

I leave Mick and Dan, up their elbows in grease and parts as they fix a broken water pump outside in the morning chill. I follow the tyre tracks I'd made yesterday afternoon as the rising sun shoots fire across the sandy landscape and five roos bounce away from the track into the emptiness. Riding off the tar-seal is such a great experience, I promise myself I'll try to do more of it in the future. After eggs and bacon in Winton, I'm away, heading west for Mount Isa and another interview arranged by Lisa back in Longreach.

Percy's 38 horses propel me along the road, which climbs up and down low, rocky outcrops the colour of gingerbread, with western USA-style escarpments in the distance.

I pass an Akubra-hatted farmer, fixing a fence, his ute parked nearby and lift my left hand in greeting. He doesn't wave back, instead taking off his hat and wiping his brow with his forearm. At the tiny Kynuna Roadhouse, I fuel-up and am served by an emaciated, toothless and grumpy old man whose legs protrude from his stubbies like two pipe-cleaners. The coffee is so bad that I leave most of

it on the formica table for the flies to die in. It's heating up outside and must already have hit the predicted high of 30 degrees.

Another 100 ks up the road I stop for a photo in McKinlay, made famous by the Walkabout Creek Hotel featured in the 1986 movie, *Crocodile Dundee*. It's now a big tourist drawcard but I don't go inside – I can be a bit snobby like that sometimes. Ten klicks up the road I curse myself for not going in for a look but by then I think it's too much effort to do a U-turn.

Cloncurry, where I have a forgettable sandwich and coffee in an Asian bakery, is located at the junction of the Matilda and Flinders Highways. The town has a real frontier vibe to it but after a walk up and down its hot main street, I feel I've got to take all my riding gear off or leave – so choose the latter.

Mt Isa or, "The Isa" is the commercial centre for north-west Queensland and boasts one of the most productive single mines (Mt Isa Mines) in the history of the world, mining lead, silver, copper and zinc. But not without a cost. A 2008 Queensland health report found that 10% of local children had blood lead levels above World Health Organisation recommendations. Monstrous chimney stacks gradually appear as I re-enter civilisation.

With 578 dusty kilometres completed, I park up and enter the cool of the KFC in the centre of town. I've been told by some kids up the road that if I sit at the far end, I can use the Westpac Bank's wi-fi and they're right. Across from me is a drop-dead gorgeously-coiffed young woman wolfing-down chicken from a bucket as though she hasn't eaten for days. She wears a voluminous yellow scarf that could double as a sheet and is puffed up at her throat like a huge cravat. Beside her, and not eating is a middle-aged chap with skin the colour of leather, dressed for the office with highly polished pointy shoes. He catches my eye and nods. In the corner a group of Aboriginal teenagers are horsing around and slurping out of huge paper cups.

An hour later I meet Joyce at an empty house she plans to move into soon. Promising to return in the morning for a chat, she allows me to make a cosy little nest of an inflatable mattress and sleeping bag on the floor in one of the empty rooms. After a welcome shower I wander down to the Buffs Club in town which is an RSL club in all but name. As promised, Joyce returns in the morning and we sit in the empty kitchen on two deck chairs I found in the garage and have a yarn.

Lady from the Bush
Joyce Scobie

Joyce was born in Alice Springs and spent her early childhood on Hidden Valley Station in the Northern Territory. She then moved to Mallapunya Station, on the Barkly Tablelands, where she married into the Darcy family who had owned the famous station since the 1920s. I start by simply asking her about her early life in the bush.

"It wasn't all good country and sometimes my parents did it tough. The cattle often had to be taken to surrounding stations to graze and us kids, two brothers and a sister had to tail 'em."

"Tail 'em?" I ask and tell her I'm a bit of a layman and she chuckles.

"Yeah, you know, ride behind the herd. Round up the strays. But I always loved horses from an early age."

Back then her parents ran mostly short-horn cattle before Brahman were established. Joyce says they often went off exploring and would come across graves, some with crosses and some with small stone cairns. "We were scared but the blackfellas wouldn't go near 'em," she says. The older Aboriginals were very superstitious according to Joyce. She goes on, "we were camped around Borroloola one time and we could see the 'Min-Min' lights. It's this light that comes up dancing around on the flat," she explains, "people used to chase it, but we never really worked out what it was. But the blackfellas, didn't like it. They thought it was spirits or something."

Joyce's parents drove cattle between Queensland and Western Australia and everywhere in between, so Joyce learned to drive cattle trucks from an early age. "One time, Dad told me to drive the lead truck and he'd be right behind me," she says. "but by the time I got to Camooweal I looked in the mirror and there was no sign of him behind me. And the truck was making an awful noise coz the muffler had fallen off somewhere on the Borroloola stock route. I didn't know what to do. I was only about 13 years old you know." When a Police Officer pulled up behind her, she hopped out of the cab. She had her long hair rolled up under her cap and with her jeans and boots, thought she'd be taken for a young man.

"It wasn't a cop I knew, so I just walked up to him bold as brass and said, 'Can I help you Officer?'" she laughs, "well what else could I do? I didn't have a licence. Well, it was only a piece of paper anyway." He told her she'd lost a muffler and asked where she was headed. "Mt Isa," she replied, "I've got to unload the cattle tonight." The cop tells her to not stop till she got there and not to move it till it was fixed.

"Well of course, I had to be a smart arse didn't I," says Joyce, "I said, 'How can I fix it if I can't move it?' Luckily Dad caught up with me then and smoothed things over."

I ask her how she reached the pedals to drive the truck. "Well I haven't grown much since I was about 11!" she replies, "but I used to put an old saddle cloth behind me to push me up a bit and I'd look through the steering wheel."

Growing up and working on a station, Joyce and her siblings acquired many skills. "You had to be versatile," she says, "you were no good to anybody unless you could do a bit of everything."

"Back when mum and dad were droving," Joyce explains, "the seasons were pretty regular. We didn't have the floods we get now.

Mustering would start around March and we'd be away sometimes for six months."

She remembers taking cattle to Western Australia when she was a kid. Her mum was driving the truck at the front, while the kids were on horses bringing up the rear. "Well suddenly mum stopped coz there was a huge croc on the track. It was a monster. We didn't know how it got there because dad said we were 40 miles from water. I don't know if he was having a go at me or what, but it was a long way between rivers. We had some blackfellas with us and of course they wanted to eat the tail," she says.

"Have you ever eaten it?"

"Yeah," she replies, "just like chicken. Anyway, dad shot him, and six men couldn't get him onto the truck, so we had to cut him up on the spot. He was a big bugger."

Joyce tells another story of when they were living at Hidden Valley Station and she was with her mum in the kitchen cooking tea. Five of her cousins were staying at the time and playing in the saddle shed.

"Anyway, we turned around and there's this Aboriginal bloke who worked for us standing in the doorway. He's just standing there staring at us with a spear in one hand and two boomerangs in the other. All he's wearing are a pair of old shorts which looked like a loincloth. Mum says, 'what do you want Cloud?' and he looked straight at mum and says, 'I'm gonna get you!"

Joyce's father was away getting a bogged truck out of a creek, where it was stuck. "Anyway," Joyce continues, "he went mad and came towards us with his spear, so mum threw a pot of boiling water at him."

Joyce's mum always carried a .38 revolver which she wore on her hip, but she'd placed in on a bench while she cooked. The Police were a long way away, Joyce points out, "and you never knew who was going to come. So, he takes off like a scalded cat," she says, "and mum tells me go get the kids and keep running till you find dad. So, I get them and take off running like the wind, down the hill, through the gate, into the scrub a bit and then we hear this noise and start climbing these bullwaddy trees. And these trees a very dense you know? So, we're climbing these bloody things and I'm pushing my little brother up ahead of me coz he's not goin' fast enough and the noise is getting closer. And then below us we see mum galloping off on a horse, so we climb down, shaking with fright and take off again through the bush.

"Sounds like the Wild West" I say, and she laughs, "well it was!"

Joyce and her cousins finally catch up with her father, who heads off in search of Cloud but doesn't manage to find him. Seven or so years later Joyce met up with Cloud again who was working on a Station next to Mallapunya. "I came out onto the veranda of the house and he was sitting there," says Joyce.

"Did he recognise you?"

"I didn't give him a chance," she replies, "I grabbed my shot gun and told him, 'see this thing, get going or I'll shoot it!

 Most Aboriginal people were fine," she explains, "but some, like Cloud could 'kick up'. How we came to get him see, we'd have the Police or the Rodeo phone us and say they had a 'wild one' they couldn't control, and would we be willing to give them 'a go' and we'd say, 'righto' and give them a job at the stock camp."

I ask Joyce if, when she was young she ever came across Aboriginals still living the way they had for thousands of years. "I know

mum and dad did but by the time I came along most of them were pretty much settled. But they still used to go Walkabout every year."

"And how long would they be gone?" I ask. "Well it varied," Joyce replies, it depended on how long the water lasted. They wouldn't do it in the dry, it was usually at the end of the year."

The Aboriginal workers would sometimes take young Joyce with them, searching for bush tucker. She explains that it was very regional, and the food varied tremendously from place to place and I wonder why I'm surprised when I consider the diversity of Australia. "I'd go with the women and we'd find bush carrots and cucumbers and wild bananas. But they weren't that safe with fires. If they caught a kangaroo of goanna, they'd just make a fire and throw the whole thing onto the flames; they didn't dress it or anything like that. If they caught fish at Mallapunya, they'd wait till the fire had burned down to coals and chuck them on. There was no wasted effort. And if they caught one when they weren't hungry, they'd half cook it, so it wouldn't go bad later."

Joyce left the land in 1985 and moved to Mt Isa, which she reckons has gone rapidly down hill lately with water restrictions. "It's just a dust bowl now," she says, "It used to be so much brighter with lovely gardens when we could rely on the rains. It's so sad. You drive round now and it's all doom and gloom and long faces." I know Joyce has to go soon and I suspect she's also dying for a cigarette, so I ask my final question, "Do you miss the bush Joyce?"

"Yeah. I'd go back tomorrow if I could. It was so free and easy back then. But I've got a bad heart, so I can't go too far."

It's been a real education talking to Joyce, who's photo I take beside my loaded bike before I head off into the bush myself.

I've been having trouble starting Percy in the morning lately and I'm a bit concerned. It turns over but just won't fire. After five minutes rest, I try again, and it reluctantly starts. Before leaving town, I pop into the information centre. "Can I buy a map of the Northern Territory?" I ask the grey-haired little lady behind the counter.

"No love, but you can have this one for free!" she says and hands me one with a flourish. In the car park I meet Dutchman Kevin who's 25 but looks 18 and is, I'd imagine, quite a hit with the young ladies. He's riding around Queensland and the NT on a Honda Transalp, a bike I've always admired, which he bought in Cairns. He plans to ride to Darwin, then fly to Timor and back to renew his tourist visa and continue his riding. He travels on a shoestring, camping free in the bush and cooking all his meals. He has everything but the kitchen sink on his battered Honda, which has over 80,000 kms on the clock. He admires the neatly packed kit on my bike. "Riding is my freedom," he says, "and I never want to stop," before wishing me bon voyage and heading for the info centre to use their shower. I smile as I head off, remembering a younger version of myself expressing similar sentiments but knowing that life will get in the way for Kevin eventually.

On the outskirts of town, I pull into a road train depot on a whim and ask a driver if I can take a photo of Percy in front of his rig, which is idling and pouring its heat into the already hot morning. Hayden, it turns out is the depot manager and invites me in for a coffee and a chat. Originally from Manchester, he moved out here in 2008 and fell in love with the place. He says he went from a life in Formula 1 Racing and the movie business, to working on cattle stations, driving road trains and now managing this place (and a lot in between I've no doubt). "This really is the lucky country George," he says and before I leave, kindly gives me some contacts in Darwin if I get short of interviews.

The barren land I'm riding through now used to be home to the Kalkadoon people who weren't quite as lucky as Hayden. They bravely resisted white settlement in a series of guerrilla-style wars until 1884, when they suffered terrible losses at Battle Mountain, from which they would never recover. Like the Native Americans half-a-world away, they inevitably succumbed to European greed and expansion that could not be stopped. It's amazing for me, born in England to realise what a young nation Australia is, as the events at Battle Mountain took place only four or five generations ago.

The next 154 kilometres (now on the Overlanders Way) go by

in a flash, as the metronomic whine of my engine lulls me into a white-line trance, interrupted only by some dead roos that I swerve around. In Camooweal, which was an important customs outpost on the Queensland border before Federation I fuel-up as the next servo is 263 ks away. I look for the romantic bush town I'd heard about but ride on, disappointed and soon cross into the Northern Territory, remembering to put my watch back 30 minutes. The speed limit is now 130 KPH and I defy any motorcyclist not to open up the throttle once past the signs. I do, but it's not long before I settle back down to a far more comfortable 110.

To occupy my mind for the rest of the day's ride, I pick the five best England football teams since 1966. I'm torn between putting Manchester City legend Colin Bell in the best team but finally put him in the second, figuring that a midfield of Scholes, Charlton, Keegan and Gascoigne cannot be beaten.

I decide to camp under a coolibah tree (like the Jolly Swagman in Waltzing Matilda) at the excellent Barkly Homestead – a bargain at only $15. The Roadhouse's facilities are marvellous, with a restaurant and bar, where I while away the evening with dozens of grey nomads listening to a long-haired Londoner, who resembles Willie Nelson, sing country music. I chat for a while with an older motorcyclist riding a BMW GS 1100. "You married?" John from Darwin asks, and I nod. "Where's the missus?"

"In Christchurch working," I reply. "Best place for 'er!" he replies.

After about an hour's riding in the morning through good grazing

country, the Barkly Highway comes to an end at one of Australia's best-known junctions. I turn right and head north for Darwin on the Stuart Highway.

Filling up at the Three Ways Roadhouse, I must leave my driver's licence at the counter with a Welsh backpacker before I can use the bowser. "Bit wetter where you're from," I say as he makes me a too-milky coffee. "I've been dreaming of rain these past six weeks," he says in his sing-song lilt.

"Well you can keep dreaming for a bit longer yet," drawls a tattooed trucker with a long nicotine-stained, blonde beard at the next table.

Back on the road I ride on the centre line whenever possible to give me a split- second extra, should any wildlife cross the road. I watch the approaching vehicles to see if the driver's wave. About half do. One lady waves at me with her pink fly swatter. Truckers don't wave unless I wave first.

An artist friend of the family and neighbour from New Zealand has given me a heart-shaped rock from the big, braided Rakaia River to place somewhere in the bush. I choose an area of red anthills about half way between Tennant Creek and Daly Waters. Climbing off Percy, I hike about 50 metres into the bush and place it on top an anthill. So, thanks Kim, there's now a little piece of New Zealand in the outback!

Somebody forgot to tell the Northern Territory that it's winter because it's stinking hot. So whenever a rest area appears, I take advantage and sit at the table in the shade. I couldn't imagine doing this trip in the summer.

In the Highway town of Elliot, a group of Aboriginal women and children have taken advantage of a large shaded area under some gum trees. The general store isn't particularly inviting but I stop anyway, like other travellers, drawn to this tiny pocket of infrastructure like a magnet. As I eat a cold Mars Bar and an apple, an Aboriginal lady wearing a ripped rugby jersey, with a baby on her hip buys a carton of VB and a pie.

Back on the Highway, the car ahead, a dented and dusty Subaru station wagon full of laughing kids, is weaving all over the road. I give it a wide berth and a dirty look as I overtake. It makes me think that perhaps autonomous vehicles aren't such a bad idea after all! And with the crazy rate of change in the modern world I figure we should get used to the idea anyway, with Toyota and the other big guys pumping billions into research and development. 'Interesting times," says my inner narrator as I twist my throttle and listen to my big single growl like an angry grizzly bear.

The Daly Waters Pub, just off the Highway, where I park up for the day is a place I've often heard travellers talk about. I climb off Percy with a sigh and book a very basic room for the night – four bunk beds all to myself and paper-thin walls. In the pub is an amaz-

ing collection of paraphernalia that travellers have donated over the years, I suppose to show that they'd been here. Bras, bank notes, flip-flops, coins, badges, road signs, old photos and God knows what else adorn the walls of the bar.

During the 1930s the town served as a refuelling point for Qantas international flights. All that remains today are a few houses, some humorous tourist curiosities and the famously iconic pub.

After unpacking, I ride back about a kilometre (Yes, I know, I should probably have walked) to where the 'Stuart Tree' is located. There is supposed to be a faint 'S' carved into the trunk, but I can't find it. It's believed to have been put there by explorer John Mc-Douall Stuart while becoming the first European to traverse the continent from south to north in 1861-62. The Stuart Highway, (known to locals as 'The Track') running from Port Augusta in South Australia, 2,834 kilometres to Darwin is named after this Scott, whose bravery and determination I can only wonder at. I'm briefly joined by three Asian girls in a hire car who are so underwhelmed by the tree, they don't even leave their vehicle.

Stretching my legs back at the pub later I meet a rather large chap on the main street sitting on a mobility scooter with "Daly Waters Highway Patrol" on the front and "Wide Load" on the back. Luckily, I have my camera and Dictaphone on me and ask if he'd mind being interviewed. I reckon it would have been rude not to.

Bush Business Man
Tim Carter

Tim Carter is just the kind of colourful, larger-than-life (not just metaphorically) Aussie character I love chatting with. He owns the IGA supermarket down in the opal mining town of Coober Pedy in South Australia. He also owns the liquor store, post office, hardware store and BP servo! "The town was dying, George. People can still make a quid with the opals but not the big money they used to. But we invested in the town, we didn't take the money and run. They say there's 1300 living there but it's more like 3000. They're all off the books."

Tim says he's always been a grafter. Born in the copper-mining town of Wallaroo on South Australia's York Peninsula, he started out as a young bloke rabbit-trapping and shooting and selling ducks. His parents were butchers, so he was always in the slaughterhouse, helping out. After a stint working on the oil rigs and then humping bags of wheat, he became an apprentice panel beater. "I soon got out of that game though because I was too rough," he says.

His family then moved to the railway town of Peterborough in South Australia, one of only three, triple-gauge-railway junction towns in the country where they bought the town's garage. "People would come into the garage and asking for a Motel all the time," Tim says, so we decided to have a crack at building one." Not content with one, the family soon owned five in the area. "You don't mind having a go do you Tim?"

"Yeah. I was only 23 at the time. But it was all borrowed money – we mortgaged Grandpa's house, well he was dead so didn't really have any choice." Later Tim bought the supermarket in Peterborough as well as a couple of farms near Naracoorte and another supermarket in Mt Gambier.

Him and his kids also ran a contracting business maintaining the natural gas pipeline for Santos Limited out of Moomba. "We had about 30 people working for us there," he says, "and while I was up there the uranium mine came along, so we did contract work on the roads for them, and next thing we started running the camp for the 160 workers up there."

I shake my head, a bit stunned. "He laughs, "yeah, I should be about 300 years old!"

Then Tim read that the historic Daly Waters pub was on the market. "I says to my wife, 'd 'you know, I might go up there and have a look.' And she says, 'don't be so bloody stupid.' So, we hopped in the car and 20 hours later we arrived here for a look round."

He obviously liked what he saw. Tim purchased the Daly Waters Pub recently, a year after checking it out. This he explains, is his usual *modus operandi*, allowing him time to assess the business and sort himself out. "I said to the kids, who are good, hard-working kids, 'what d'you reckon?' and we thought it'd make a great project, so that's why we're here now."

Tim obviously speaks to a lot of people and has his finger on the pulse. "People are demanding more and more these days," he says, "the whole grey nomad-baby boomer thing is a huge industry in Australia now. Everyone is on the road. Little shops are closing thanks to the internet and so many people are getting shafted these days. I think a lot of them are saying, 'to hell with the modern world, we're going on the road.'"

We agree that the world is going to hell-in-a-handbasket. Maccas, KFC, The Warehouse, Walmart, etc come in to town and before you know it, the high street is boarded-up. The fat cats get richer while a few locals might be employed on the minimum wage. "I've seen it happen is Surfers Paradise," says Tim, "the big boys came in, shops became vacant and nobody wants to go near vacant shops. Soon the town centre's buggered." Tim is now on a roll. "I think the Government has forgotten about the little people – the ones from the bush who built this country. We had the prime minister in Tennant Creek last week saying, 'We'll fix the Aboriginal problem.' Bullshit! He'll do nothing."

Tim is currently spending $300,000 on a new sewage system at the pub. "There's nothing worse than having to push a turd down the pipe at night-time with a bunch of kids watching you," he says. In the wet season Daly Waters can receive three inches of rain in an hour and the main street and pub are often flooded out. Just up the road is a flying fox that's used to send groceries across the flooded

river. "But it's beautiful and green up here in the wet," Tim says, "hot though, and the humidity is worse than the tropics. And we get thousands of wallabies come in from the bush. There's a couple over there," and he points to where two wallabies are grazing nearby in the dusk.

    I nod towards the pub and ask Tim what his plans are. Things are really rocking across the road, with country music and the happy chatter of customers spilling into the early evening. "I just plan to keep this historic place ticking over, make it better and give customers what they want." Leaving Tim to his highway patrolling, I wander into the pub in search of a beer.

JELLYFISH SAFETY

WARNING
MARINE STINGERS MAY BE PRESENT IN THESE WATERS

SWIMMING NOT ADVISED

DANGER
BOX JELLYFISH CAN BE DEADLY

OCTOBER TO MAY
DO NOT ENTER THE SEA

JUNE TO SEPTEMBER
SERIOUS STINGS HAVE BEEN RECORDED IN ALL MONTHS OF THE YEAR

CHILDREN ARE ESPECIALLY AT RISK

CONSIDER WEARING PROTECTIVE CLOTHING

TAKE VINEGAR TO THE BEACH

FIRST AID
POUR VINEGAR LIBERALLY ON AFFECTED AREAS

PROVIDE RESUSCITATION IF NEEDED

TRANSPORT TO HOSPITAL IMMEDIATELY

Northern Territory Government

FIRST AID PRIORITIES FOR MARINE STINGS

Chapter Five.
THE NORTH

"This is the Crown Land. This is the Brown Land. This is not our Land"

Midnight Oil

I enjoy a great night at the pub, along with what must be over a hundred grey nomads, whose rigs are parked out the back, along with a few locals. The beer flows and barramundi and chips are wolfed down as we listen to Tom Maxwell, "Voice of the Bush" who has an old time, Slim Dusty vibe to him.

A bearded trucker of around 60 called Pete, with whiskers like a white wire brush and eyebrows to match is holding forth at the bar. He's wearing the uniform of tattered blue singlet, stubbies and boots (no socks interestingly) and rests his can of beer on the ledge of his belly. His baseball cap looks as though it would need to be surgically removed. I squeeze into the small semi-circle of drinkers in time to catch his joke. "So, 80-year-old Bert, a retired cockie always wanted a pair of fancy new boots see," he begins. "So, he finally buys a pair and wears them home. He swaggers into the lounge and asks his wife Marge if she notices anything different. Marge looks up from her knitting and looks him up and down and says, 'nope.' So, Bert storms out to the bathroom then walks back in completely naked except for his new boots. 'Notice anything different now Marge?' he asks a bit louder. Marge looks him up and down again and says, 'Bert, what's different? It's hanging down today and it'll be hanging down tomorrow!'" Pete pauses for another swig of beer, before continuing, "So, furious, Burt says, 'd 'you know why it's hanging down Marge? It's hanging down coz it's looking at my new boots!' Without missing a beat Marge replies, "well ya shoulda bought a new hat Bert. Shoulda bought a new hat.'" We all erupt in laughter, even the young Czech couple who don't speak good English and Pete burps contentedly before turning in for the night.

In the morning Percy is reluctant to start. I almost drain the battery before he roars into life. It's a bit of a worry. I re-join the Stuart Highway and head for Darwin. On either side of me is The Bush. Supremely indifferent to me, my motorcycle and this miniscule strip of tarmac that represents civilization. Above me, the huge vault of sky, a burnished and flawless blue. The sheer immensity of it makes me feel small and insignificant and I think it's healthy to laugh at any perceived sense of self-importance. In his excellent book The Bush, Don Watson says, "……the life it harbours is the life of the Australian mind. It is, by many accounts, the source of the Nation's idea of itself."

At Mataranka, famed for its thermal pools and palm forest, I eat a home-made meat pie for breakfast that contains nothing but super-heated gravy. I sit in the shade of a tree and try not to make a mess down my leather jacket while chatting to a pleasant biker couple from Brisbane, who are also heading for Darwin, him on a Harley and her riding a red Ducati.

I'm now in the real heart of Never Never country, made famous (or reasonably well known anyway) by Jeannie Gunn who wrote her classic, *We of the Never Never* on nearby Elsey Station in 1902.

It's a new experience to follow behind the Brisbane couple as far as Katherine, through land that is increasingly forested. I watch, off to my left and behind a stock fence, a huge mob of cattle trot in single file through the bush. The grass strips on either side of the road are blackened by fire and in some cases still burning. I discover later that it's the result of deliberate burning to get rid of invasive, non-indigenous grasses. In Katherine my new friends ride on with a wave, while I take advantage of the first Wi-Fi for 1300 k's, sit in the air-conditioned comfort of the Public Library for a while and catch up on my emails.

Further up the Stuart Highway, I sit under a fan and enjoy a cold one in the Pine Creek Motel. Two thin, brown diggers in work clothes and bush hats are well into their cups at the bar discussing giving up smoking. "Well you need a 2nd mortgage to buy a pack of smokes anyways," says one. "Yeah," his mate agrees, "don't ask me to give the grog away but."

Back on the road there are not only a few clouds but some low undulating hills as well. And even a passing lane or two. And some decidedly tropical looking trees called sand-palms mixed with thousands of red anthills, some taller than a man. Another 150-odd k's of tarmac pass beneath my boots before I stop at Adelaide River, where I fuel up and have another drink in the shade of the Hotel. A young English couple fuel up beside me. They're doing a whole lap of Australia having started in WA's Margaret River. He's on a Triumph Tiger, while she rides a trusty KLR 650. I congratulate her on her taste and she smiles. I have a quick walk around the neat, simple and peaceful War Cemetery where 434 Australian, Canadian and British servicemen who died in the region in World War 11 are buried.

About 60 k's shy of Darwin I turn left to ride to the top of the Cox Peninsula, where I'm staying with a friend and work colleague of my brother-in-law Ken "Tuna Boy" Banwell. It's a magic ride on a lovely twisty (it's all relative but any bends now are "twisty") and empty road. The vegetation has morphed imperceptibly from dry scrub at Three Ways to the now lush, tropical vegetation of the far north.

I receive a wonderful welcome from Robin "Crocko" Croxson and his wife Barbara when I arrive at their home in a gorgeous bush setting at Wagait Beach. I'm treated like the prodigal son and am soon ensconced, glass in hand on the back veranda, listening to the sound of the sea beyond their strip of bush that runs down to the beach.

We share tales of my brother-in-law Ken of which there are always plenty. I tell a funny one of when Ken and I were touring Japan on motorcycles in 2006.

After a long day in the saddle, we had found this tiny drinking establishment in a small town on the north west coast of Honshu. Earlier in the day Ken and I had been shooting the breeze and talking movies and he (mainly on the strength of having a similarly shaved head) fancied himself as a bit of a Bruce Willis lookalike. I think my response was along the lines of, "dream on!"

Ken, who lived in Japan for 20 years, is comfortabley sitting cross legged on a cushion, but I can't quite manage it. "Campai!" he says, and we clink glasses of beer, "cheers!"

At the next table are a group of old timers, three sheets to the wind and merrily singing. They are amiable drunks and are part of a Martial Arts Convention and we don't mind when one of them ambles over to join us. He had been eyeing us up and down since we'd entered. He orders more beer for us and sake for himself, a typical act of hospitality, I'd become accustomed to in Japan. His English isn't great, but he manages to tell us that he is over 70 and is a black belt 6th Dan in Aikido. He feels my right bicep and strokes my beard approvingly. "You," he says, with his beery breath, "Crint Eastwood," and slaps my back. I nod, approvingly. That'll do me!

"Your friend," he says, beaming at Ken, who is just waiting for the Bruce Willis comparison. There's a long pause as our mate studies Ken's face with a gleam in his eye................. "Alfled Hitchcock!" and makes the glasses jump as he slaps the table for emphasis. My new friend and I fall over laughing (not hard as we're on the floor anyway) while Ken gulps his beer and shakes his head in disgust!

Opportunist
Robin "Crocko" Croxson

When Rob was nine years old his mother and American GI father separated. His mother left the USA and moved back to Britain with the kids, quickly followed by his father, who tried at knife point to wrest young Rob back from her clutches. "I remember," says Rob, "him turning up at the caravan where we lived. We had no money at the time and were living on jam sandwiches. As a consequence, us kids were made wards of the court which wasn't lifted till mum was re-married."

A month before his GCE 'O' Level exams, he was sent from their home in the midlands to stay with his Auntie in Somerset as his mother's second marriage had failed. "My mum caught him rooting a Shakespearean actress from Stratford upon Avon," says Rob with a chuckle.

It was so disruptive to his education that Rob said, "fuck it" and left school to work on a building site. "Whilst I'd demonstrated plenty of aptitude, I had no qualifications," says Rob in his very cultured tones. His stint as a hod-carrier didn't last long so he decided to join

the Royal Air Force. After a three-day aptitude test, the Wing Commander (complete with handlebar moustache) sat him down. "We have a place for you Croxson. In what capacity would you like to join the Air Force?" he asked. Rob told him he'd quite like to be a pilot or a navigator but when he was offered a job as a cook, he decided to join the Army instead.

"So, in 1965 I joined the Parachute Regiment," he says.

After a year Rob damaged his right foot in training and transferred to the regular army in the BAOR (British Army of the Rhine.) Because of his para experience he became part of the ACE Mobile Force, which was a highly mobile unit designed to defend the flanks of NATO. "I wasn't a very good soldier. I was frustrated at my lack of prospects due to my lack of education," says Rob, "I used to get into a bit of strife and bounced around a bit rank wise."

One day, a bored Rob decided to borrow an army vehicle, complete with Bren gun mounted on the roof and drive it to Hamburg to see his girlfriend. The authorities not surprisingly took a dim view of this, as Hamburg was a de-militarised zone. "Well they banged me up and I was looking at a possible Court Martial. I had a bit of a bad reputation at this stage and had some bad mates, who organised a jail break. So of course, once of the stockade I 'borrowed' another vehicle to visit my girlfriend again."

Gunner Croxson was soon staring down the barrel of several guns held by the German civilian KRIPO (CID equivalent) and found himself back in jail facing further charges. But instead of a Court Martial he was sent to military corrective training in an effort to divert his obvious energy into something positive.

Corrective training complete, the Battery Commander had him in his office. "Well Croxson, now you have all that behind you, I'm going to send you on NCO (non-commissioned officer) training. Will you come top of the course?" he asked.

"And I did," Rob says. "I was promoted on the parade ground to Lance Bombardier, in the Royal Horse Artillery, given a big red sash, a swagger stick and silver bugle and saw my time out at that level. But all in all, I did enjoy it."

With that Rob gets up and hands me his swagger stick. "Would it be fair to say you had problems with authority Rob?"

"Maybe a little bit," he says with a grin.

Rob was de-mobilised with his little red book, listing qualifications and testimonials. His Commander, who Rob says, hated his guts but was required to paint him in the best light commented that, 'Lance Bombardier Croxson is a bright and likeable young NCO capable of supervising mediocre tasks.'

"He was right, though wasn't he?" says Barbara as she brings us some more of Rob's home brew, which isn't bad at all.

After leaving the army in 1972 a mate of Rob's got him a start as a pest controller with the Public Health Department in Royal Leamington Spa. "Ronny and I would work hard till 11.30 am, then retire to the Gauntlet or the Green Man and enjoy an extended eight-pint business lunch which would take us through till about 3.30, when we'd pour ourselves back into the company van and sign off for the day."

Two years later, in 1974 Rob emigrated to Australia, arriving in Sydney with a couple of hundred quid in his pocket. "I had no particular ambition," he says, "I just wanting to get as far away from England as possible. I promptly got a job selling filing cabinets and so forth which was great for the first six months as I got a car, a salary and if I got around to selling anything, a bit of commission."

Rob says he increasingly found himself in the company of professional people like barristers, solicitors and accountants. He apparently had a marvellous English accent, which when added to his 'gift of the gab' seemed to carry some credibility. "I soon found myself employed as a foot-soldier, 3-piece suit and crocodile skin briefcase in hand, pounding up and down the CBD's of Sydney and

Melbourne flogging tax minimisation schemes."

"My role," he explains, "was to draw attention and hook someone in, then hand it over to the experts. Basically, instead of paying 48 cents in the dollar, they paid our fee and we purchased their tax liability; I won't bore you with the details. The fun aspect was that I ended up living in this mansion in Melbourne which doubled as a high-class brothel. I formed quite a sibling-like relationship with the working girls actually."

Things went swimmingly for a while till the then Treasurer John Howard, got wind of these schemes and introduced retrospective legislation. "So, what we were doing yesterday quite legally was suddenly deemed illegal. I remember receiving a tax assessment saying I owed 12 million dollars," he shakes his head as I raise my eyebrows, "which of course I had no reasonable expectation of paying." Rob was advised by experts to avoid bankruptcy by inviting the Tax Department to a meeting and say, 'listen, you want 12 million. All I have is $500. How much of that do you want?'

To cut a long story short, his $500 offer was accepted, and Rob moved on to another chapter. "A couple of mates of mine and my step-father had acquired this antique business. They didn't have much of a clue and were running in into the ground. I had a few bob so I thought I'd try and breath some life back into it."

"Did you know anything about antiques?"

"Not much George, but I never let little details like that stand in my way."

It wasn't long before Rob and his new partners were running a very successful business out of their 10,000 square foot warehouse in Sydney's Balmain, with a dozen employees, buying, fixing up and selling furniture. He'd travel far and wide, often buying up entire businesses. Rob says it was a steep learning curve initially, but they were happy days. "My working life up to that point had always been kind of hand to mouth but now I had a sort of stability."

They also bought a lot of demolition material including dozens of inch and a quarter thick marble slab partitions from the toilets of the 1920's Hordern building. There were many damaged Victorian tables sitting in the Balmain workshop, which Rob, ever the opportunist, decided to put the slabs of marble onto to create beautiful marble topped tables.

"We were churning them out," he says, "there was one memorable incident when we were delivering one to a surgeon in Mossman. It took six of us to lift this bloody thing. Anyway, as we were carrying it out of the truck, the sunlight caught the marble at a certain angle and we could see scratched into it all these filthy toilet comments about blow jobs, arses, tits and cocks, etc. My mate, said, 'what are we gonna do about this Crocko? First time they spill some red wine on this it will all come to light.' I said, 'just keep fuckin' walking!'"

As we laugh, Barbara points into the dusk and we see a small wallaby hop away towards the beach.

Rob spent a lot of his spare time fishing off Bermagui on the south coast from a little game fishing boat he'd bought. So, when he tired of the antique business he sold his share and moved down there permanently. In typical Crocko fashion he knew he could catch fish so decided he'd like to do it for a living. In another steep learning curve Rob spent four years and went through four boats before he really started catching fish for the local and export market. "I was then seduced with the notion of catching a good tuna, looking after it correctly, putting a bit of lippy on it, sending it business class to Tokyo and getting a million dollars per fish."

Rob soon became one of the pioneers of the fresh chilled sashimi market, getting the fish into Japan within 72 hours of being caught. Yet another steep learning curve! "As with most pioneers," he says, "the first ones usually get a lot of arrows in the arse."

Rob got in at the start of the burgeoning tuna industry on the NSW coast and despite being "ripped off by the middle men," embraced it and enjoyed some great results all through the 80's.

Not one to rest on his laurels, Rob's next venture had him selling up and buying into a fishing venture in Fiji where he went to live for two years, heading up a fishing operation which unfortunately went the way all foreign investments go in Fiji. "They play the dumb islanders," Rob explains, "allow you to bring your assets in and then make it very difficult for you when you want out. You basically have to leave your assets behind Thank you very much. We even had the Prime Minister on our board of directors but it didn't do any good."

Returning to Bermagui, Rob then managed a state-of-the-art Korean fish exporting facility, while also driving one of their boats, an 80-foot Tasmanian cray boat that was so impervious to weather it could manage 25 sea days per month. "Then in typical Korean fashion, as soon as I'd taught them all they thought they needed to know they sacked me."

Ever the entrepreneur, Rob decided to set up in opposition to them and it wasn't long before his company, Mariserv became successful. "We had our own trucks and would pick up the fish from the boats and use the export facilities in Narooma, Nelson Bay and Sydney. We also supplied the boats with ice and fuel, like a wharf side valet service. We then purchased our own premises in Coffs Harbour which to this day is one of the top export facilities along the coast."

That's when Rob met my brother-in-law Ken who was importing tuna into the Tokyo fish markets working for TandF fish importers. "The very first shipment I sent to TandF was 20 tonnes of yellowfin tuna out of Coffs Harbour." Rob says.

Ken then suggested Rob (who was getting sick of driving up and down the NSW coast) go to Papua New Guinea to help set up the tuna boats for a new company. This he did, as well as showing them how to grade and look after the fish. This then turned into a separate consultancy business and next thing he knew he was flying to the Seychelles, Mauritius, Tonga, Sri-Lanka and the Maldives, ending with a seven-month stint in Cape Town.

Ten years ago, Barbara had a cancer scare. "One thing it brings home to you in those situations," says Rob, "when a family member gets cancer, everyone has to deal with it." Barbara responded well to treatment and the prognosis was good so, selling up their businesses on the east coast, they decided it was time for a sea change.

Rob eventually landed a job in Darwin with a charter fishing operation. For the next three years he captained their 75-foot luxury mother ship, while Barbara was employed as the chef. "It was high end stuff. We had four, 4.7 metre dingys on the roof with a professional fishing guide and two punters in each boat. We'd cruise all along the north coast and Kimberley region, catching barramundi in the mangroves. We had a ball, but eventually I got sick of un-blocking the seven vacuum flush toilets. That rather took the glamour out of it."

There then followed a fascinating couple of years with Rob skippering boats for a commercial dive operation, involved in laying the 900-kilometre gas pipeline out the north west cape. "During this time," Rob says, "we discovered almost a thousand magnetic anomalies that had to be investigated. This eventuated into another job driving dive platforms for marine archaeologists. We found some great stuff; old pearling gear and Second World War stuff. We preserved the lot for posterity. After identifying artefacts, archaeologists would wrap them, and we'd place them back on the Ocean floor in an area like a huge filing cabinet for future reference. It's all there to this day."

After a stint at driving the local ferry to Darwin and the Tiwi Islands, Rob landed his current job which he does on a part time, casual basis. "I became a trainer, training people to be ship's masters, coxswains and engineers," he pauses to show me some photos of him and his high-viz clad students. "We teach short courses like radio operation, survival at sea, stuff like that. Sometimes I'll spend a week in Jabiru in the Kakadu National Park teaching the Aboriginal Sea Rangers to drive the boats they'd already been driving for years. The Aboriginal people are great to work with. They get the jokes before anybody else, they're pretty sharp. Not much gets past them. What some people see as solemn disregard is actually shyness and if you take the time to talk to them and crack a joke, their faces will just light up."

There are obviously countless untold stories in Rob's life, some x-rated and others I've no room for (such as a stint gold prospecting and playing bass guitar in a band called The Riddled Liver Band) and he really deserves a whole book. I ask Rob to sum up his life so far. "Bullshit George," he shrugs, "always baffles brains."

I enjoy a relaxing few days with Rob and Barbara. One morning as I eat my toast on the veranda, I catch a glimpse of a sand coloured animal, I think is a dingo. Rob confirms it, "yeah, sometimes they take pet dogs," he says. I catch the 12- minute Mandorah ferry into Darwin (130 k's if I went by road) every morning to wander around in the 33-degree heat. It's obviously unrecognisable to the place I visited back in 1981 and is now a buzzing, multi-ethnic little city with spacious thoroughfares and manicured lawns. I can even find a decent coffee. The first morning, I ask a bloke for directions into the town centre. "I'm going that way," he says in a Glaswegian

accent, "I'll walk wi' ye."

John McCready, in his late 60's is fit and tanned and dressed for the heat in shorts and sandals. He'd travelled up from his home in Coober Pedy and has been here for three months. He tells me he's a singer and is just travelling around for a bit to rest his voice. "People are just too busy to talk to each other these days George," he says as we pass three old Aboriginal men, all with long white beards, sitting under a tree. Out of the blue he declares that he doesn't drink, which I say is rare for a Glaswegian. "Well, I watched friends and family drink themselves to death and I said, 'that's no' for me,'" he pauses, "I was born in the last century ye know."

"I had a suspicion you were over 18 John," I reply, wondering where the conversation is heading next as his blue eyes hold my stare and he grins a gap-toothed smile.

We come to the pedestrian mall, bright, colourful and modern. "I'll show you a painting I just bought," says John as he takes my arm and darts into a shop, stepping around two Aboriginal women, busy dot painting on the ground by the door. He gets the owner to show us the artwork depicting Uluru that he'd bought the day before. It's beautiful and I take a photo. "You know it was creepy," says John, "I saw this lady in the mall and just knew it was Trephina Thangawa, the artist who painted my picture!"

As we part outside the shop, John says, "d'ye know the difference between an alligator and a crocodile George?" I shake my head. "One will see ye later and one will see ye after a while," he points his finger at me like a pistol, winks and wanders off.

Next morning Rob takes me off-road for a drive into the bush in his Landcruiser. After a while, as Rob tells me more of his adventurous life, we emerge onto a huge plain where wild horses, pigs and 'roos congregate in the evening to graze. The area is dotted with enormous grey magnetic termite mounds that give the plain an, other-worldly feel. They're built from dirt and excretions on a precise north/south line to take advantage of the morning and evening sun. Rob is something of an ornithologist and makes a great guide. (I wouldn't be surprised, knowing his varied CV, to hear that he's been employed as such at some stage!) He points out mud larks, rainbow bee eaters, masked plovers, pied butcher birds and orange footed scrub foul. We also visit the remains of the B24J Liberator which crashed in the bush in 1945 while on a practice bombing mission, with the loss of six US airmen.

Next day I wander down to the beach, where a 4.3 metre 'salty' was caught two years ago. I'm warned to watch out for snakes in the leaf litter of the yard. Apparently, there are golden tree snakes, keel backs, slaty greys, coastal taipans and death adders around. The goanna population has suffered greatly in recent years due to the cane toad, which the goanna eats and promptly dies from its poison. Waigat beach is an enormous, empty crescent of golden sand, bordered by colourful rock formations. The sea looks inviting and I'd love a swim, but warnings abound of the dangers of crocs and box jellyfish. I must be content with a paddle: A knotted hanky on my head would complete the picture!

Another day, Barbara drives me (they leave a car parked at the ferry terminal in town) to the Northern Territory Museum and Art Gallery and the Military Museum where I learn about the devastation caused by Cyclone Tracy in 1975 and the 242 Japanese aircraft that attacked in 1942.

One night, Rob and Barbara's next-door neighbour Marie is invited to tea and has us enthralled with her fascinating life story. She kindly agrees to be interviewed, so in the morning I pop over, dictaphone at the ready.

Indigenous Writer
Marie Munkara

Marie was delivered by her two grandmothers on the banks of the Mainoru River in Arnhem Land. "My mum was a full blood woman, but I came out this colour," she says, indicating her coffee coloured skin.

Nanna Clara, looked at me when I was born and said, "oh, this one too white, this one.' They wanted to throw me to the crocodiles because they knew that I would be 'taken' away and not allowed to die in my 'country.'"

It's a hell of way to start your story and I'm gobsmacked, "Oh my God," is all I can say. "Fed to the crocodiles?" I'm incredulous.

Marie nods, "My other Nana, Nellie, said that I just looked up at her silently. Must be the only time in my life, I kept my mouth shut! Anyway, Nana Nellie says, 'no, we gotta let this one live coz she'll come back, this one.'

And I did! I did. I found my way home again!"

I'm still coming to grips with what I'm hearing, "excuse my ignorance Marie, but when you say, 'taken away', you're referring to the 'stolen generation stuff'?"

"So, my mother gets married off to this Tiwi man and we found ourselves living on Bathurst Island. She worked in the laundry and he was a carpenter. One day, when my mum was at work, Father Falon, took me away to the Mission on the other side of the Island with the coloured kids under some trumped up charge of 'neglect.' But there was no way I was neglected! My mum and her husband petitioned Bishop O'Lachlan to get me back, but it was no use."

At the age of three Marie was flown to Adelaide and handed over to a white couple. "When the nuns put me on the plane to Darwin, I ran up to this young, blond pilot and threw my arms around him because I thought he was my new dad," she says.

English was Marie's 5th language so the couple initially thought she was retarded. When she was older, she asked why she was a different colour and was told she was found under a gooseberry bush.

"My first memories of being in their house was of him sexually molesting me. He'd think nothing of walking past me and grabbing my breasts or sticking his hand up my skirt. Later, when I found my records, I discovered that between the age of four and six I went to Hospital three times from bleeding because of what he was doing. The doctors must have known what was going on, but they turned a blind eye. I was sent to a child psychologist, as I was obviously angry and unhappy and traumatised. At around seven or eight I said to myself, 'you've either got to sink or swim.' So, I chose to swim. I knew that one day I'd grow up and get out of there. I remember when I was 14 standing outside his bedroom door with a hammer in my hand, thinking, 'I'm going to kill him.'"

Despite Marie's churning emotions, common sense prevailed. "I told myself to be sensible. Because they went to church every Sunday and donated money to the school and were white God-fearing people. I knew that nobody would believe me, and I'd spend my life in jail."

With this, Marie gets up to make us a cuppa and I sit there a but stunned.

Marie was an able student and realised early, the value of a good education. At 16 and now living in Ballarat, she finished her final exam, collected her already packed bags and left home, taking a taxi to a friend's flat.

"When I was older, I rang his wife up and let her know how much I hated what he'd done to me and asked if she'd been aware of what was going on while I was in their care. She said, 'yes I knew but I married him for better or for worse.' I just wanted them to know that I'd never be speaking to them again and that I was disowning them," she says, "I then rang my two step-brothers and step-sister and told them what their father had been doing to me."

Marie would sometimes visit her step-sister, having checked first that her step-parents were not at home. On one of these occasions, when they were overseas, Marie, now 28 was visiting and looking on the book shelves for something to read when she made a discovery. She found a card with her date and place of birth on it. She pulled out the Atlas and discovered that the Mainoru River was in the Northern Territory. "'God!' I said to myself, 'I must be black!' because they'd always intimated that I might be from the South Pacific or something."

Marie wrote a letter to the Daly River Mission, where, according to the card, she'd been baptised, and a reply followed informing her that her real mother's name was Judy Munkara from Bathurst Island.

Bursting with enthusiasm, Marie couldn't wait to visit her real mother. She felt duty bound to inform her step-mother, who's reaction was, "Well how ungrateful. After all we've done for you! Just watch out for those shifty black people." I can only shake my head in wonder.

After a white-knuckle flight on a tiny plane from Darwin, Marie, the only passenger, eventually touches down on Bathurst Island. "I'd filled some apple juice bottles with wine," she says, "in case of emergency. It was a bit of a shock. We landed on this dirt air strip with an old tin shack. I had imagined some kind of resort with people in bikinis, sipping daiquiris. The plane left me standing there, along with some boxes."

When a battered ute pulled up, Marie asked the driver if he spoke

English and if he knew Judy Munkara. "Yes, to both questions," he replied. She sat in the back with all the boxes and bumped and rattled along the pot holes to the township. "It was like a 3rd world country, with naked children everywhere and the people were so black, George."

The driver delivers her outside a dilapidated little house. A woman walks down the steps and Marie involuntarily clutches her bag closer. She asks her who she is. "I'm your mother," she replies.

"But I couldn't believe it," says Marie, because she's short, is as black as the ace of spades and has a big afro." She's invited in for a cup of tea and Marie thinks, 'I'll go along with it as from here maybe I can find the real Judy Munkara.

There's not a stick of furniture, so they sit on the floor. Marie is handed a tin mug and wonders where she can put her mouth on it to avoid germs. Her mother drinks from a corned beef can and Marie realises she's given her mother's only cup. Sensing Marie's discomfort, it's suggested they go outside and sit under the tree in the sand.

"She then asks me if I'm hungry," says Marie, "then rustles around inside and comes out with this wallaby arm with the claw and a bit of fur still attached, which attracts the local mangy dogs." While Marie is throwing up into the bushes, she sees three old men walking down the track and she immediately recognises the middle one as her Grandfather. This man approaches her and tells her that she's grown up so beautiful.

"It's all too much and I just start crying."

"Well that was some homecoming!" I say, shaking my head again.

"It was horrific, I thought we were going on a camping trip, but we ended up sleeping on the beach. I said, 'what about crocodiles?' and my grandfather said, 'no crocs gonna come near your mum, she's too cranky that one!'

Turtles came up to lay their eggs and were promptly turned upside down, ready to eat the next day. Her Grandfather turned them back over and put them back into the water, when he saw the look of horror on Marie's face. She then got a dirty look from Auntie

Blanche who was looking forward to turtle for breakfast. Suddenly the culture shock is all too much for Marie and she tells her Grandfather that she must go. She's unceremoniously dropped off at the tiny airport without a backward glance

On the plane Marie chats to the only other passenger and discovers that she's the mother-in-law of the young blonde pilot who had flown Marie away from home all those years ago. "This is like a link in the chain," she says, "It was such a powerful omen that I knew I had to go back."

A few months later, a determined Marie (and she's nothing if not determined) sorted out her affairs, left her job at the Health Department in Melbourne and returned to Bathurst Island, where she says, nobody batted an eyelid. "They knew I'd be back," she says simply, shrugging her shoulders. She stayed in her mum's little house, sleeping on an inflatable mattress for nine months. "Nine months," she says, "almost like a re-birthing."

Marie doesn't think she would have become a writer had she not returned, and we talk of the different branches we all take in life's road and where they lead us. Finding things a bit too primitive on Bathurst Island, Marie compromised and moved to nearby Darwin, landing a job training health workers. As part of her job she is sent to Arnhem Land, where Charlie, the senior health worker says to her one day out of the blue, "so when are you going to come and visit your family?"

Thinking all this time that she was from the Tiwi Islands, Marie is confused. "You're not Tiwi," Charlie says, "your mother from this country. This is your country." So, after work one day they set off to visit Marie's family.

Charlie drives them to Uncle Wayne's place, who greets her with, "oh, finally!" They must have been forewarned because Marie's Uncle David, Uncle Jackie and Auntie Brenda are all waiting to meet her. "Look at your right foot," Uncle Wayne tells Marie and she compares her foot to theirs. They're the same. The last three toes on all their feet are distinctly short. "All us Rembarrnga people have the same toes," says Uncle Wayne, "you are Rembarrnga from western

Arnhem Land."

Marie eventually tracks her Grandfather down to a house in Beswick, near Katherine. He's a big, powerful man with white hair and sits on a veranda making a didgeridoo. "By this time," Marie says, "I've learnt some respect, so I wait for him to acknowledge me." After a while her Grandfather looks up and as Marie starts to explain herself, he says, "I know who you are."

A few weeks later Marie travels to Bulman where finds her Nana Nellie, who is her mother's father's sister. Over the next three days Marie learns the details of her birth and is taken to the very spot on the river where her Grandmothers delivered her. "It was amazing, George, I slept on the veranda with my Nana Nellie and we talked and talked, and I felt completely and utterly at home. She also told me that my dreaming was the mermaid, yawk yawk."

She also discovered that two of her uncles were assassins, whose role it was to kill anybody who broke tribal law. "My mother should have been killed for not taking her promised husband and giving birth to someone as white as me," she says, "but was repreived because she was an adored only daughter. Instead she was banished to the Tiwi Islands."

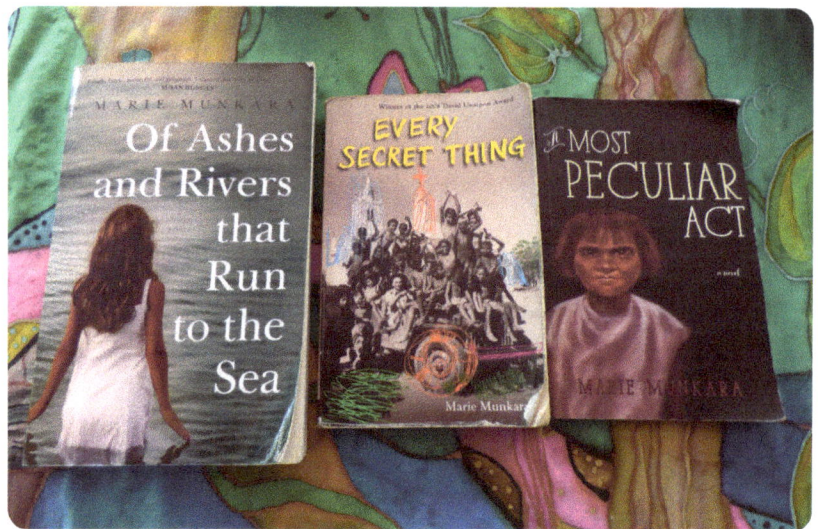

Changing the subject, I get onto writing. Marie had always been a writer. As a young girl she loved Enid Blyton's, Famous Five and Secret Seven books and liked to re-write the end of the stories.

"What about your first published book?"

"Whenever I'd be sitting with my family and they'd be talking about this and that, I'd always say that I was going to write a book about it one day. And my mother said, 'just wait till I die please.'" So that became Marie's first book, Every Secret Thing published in 2008, which she says was basically taking the piss out of the Bathurst Island Mission. "The priests sleeping with the local women, stuff like that," she says, "there were no secrets after that. But it's all fictionalised with the names changed."

Marie modestly reckons that it was all an accident and her success was handed to her. "My daughter Amber wrote a story, which her teacher entered, along with some other student's work into the Northern Territory Literary Awards and of course she goes and wins."

The NT Writer's Centre then interviews Amber and asks Marie if she was a writer too. "I was never bothered about being published," Marie says, "but I gave the Director some stuff I'd written, and she said she'd be seeing some publishers soon and would I mind if she showed them my work."

It wasn't long before Madonna Duffy of University of Queensland Press had Marie in her office. "She told me I had a gift for the absurd," says Marie and that she wanted to publish me. I didn't know what to say so I just said, 'OK'"

"I really wasn't expecting it, George. She told me to finish it off and give it to her by May or something and she'd enter it for the David Unaipon Award, which I did. As I wrote it, it was like someone else was writing through me. Anyway, I'd almost forgotten about it when a lady from the Queensland Premier's Office rang to tell me I'd won. I thought she must be talking about a raffle or something. I went, 'oh fuck. Sorry I mean oh wow!' So, I won $15,000 and was flown to Brisbane for the award ceremony." Every Secret Thing also won the 2010 Northern Territory Book of the Year.

While busy writing her next book, A Most Peculiar Act, Marie was asked to write a children's book. "But there's swearing and sex in my books, how can I write a children's book?" Marie laughs, "they told me to dump that but just keep the humour, so I spent the next three Saturday afternoons writing this children's book Rusty Brown and they liked it and asked for another one, so I wrote Rusty and Jo Jo over five Saturday afternoons."

Fiona Henderson from Penguin books then rang to ask if Marie would be interested in writing her memoir, as she'd heard stories of Marie's journey finding her home. Her mother had passed away at this stage so, after a little thought, Marie agreed and soon the words were flying onto the computer screen. In ten weeks, she'd written 86,000 words and Of Ashes and Rivers that Run to the Sea was finished. "But it was a nightmare to get edited," Marie says, "it took 17 months and five different editors!"

Her life story, told so poignantly in Of Ashes and Rivers that Run to the Sea will soon be made into a movie and she's busy working on the script for a TV mini-series based on her first book, Every Secret Thing.

"Well done you!" I say and give Marie a high five.

More scripts are in the wings and Marie has also had talks about a children's animated series for the ABC. She is so charmingly modest about her achievements and says she must constantly pinch herself as though she were dreaming. "It gives me such a thrill to see my books in book shops."

As I leave to walk back to Rob's house, I'm still shaking my head as I think about Marie's remarkable story. What a treat it was to meet such a strong and delightful lady who thoroughly deserves all her success.

When it's time to leave I'm strangely reluctant, as Rob and Barbara have made me feel so welcome. However, the siren call of the road can't be denied, and it soon has me in its thrall once more.

It's only 350 kilometres back to Katherine so I can take my time. It would be easy in this heat to ride without a jacket but memories of laying on my side in the Medical Centre while a nurse picked gravel out of my hip and elbow make me err on the side of caution and leave it on. It's a thin line between folly and logic but logic wins out (Mr Spock's voice in my head tells me I'm doing the right thing). I have made some concessions to the heat and wear my jeans instead of my riding pants and my fingerless summer gloves.

Back at Pine Creek I re-hydrate with a banana smoothie in a great little café called Maisey's, whose walls are adorned with black and white photos of old Hollywood movie stars. I take some notes and

read the local rag as Gerry Rafferty sings about a bloke who's, 'got a dream about buying some land; giving up the booze and the one-night stands.'

The Gold Rush of the 1870's put Pine Creek on the map. I potter around town for a bit, discovering an open-air exhibition of old mining machinery, as well as an old steam locomotive at the Railway Station. The Station was built in 1888 as part of the grand plan to connect Alice Springs to Darwin but was the 'end of the line' for 29 years till it was connected to Katherine.

I pull into the Katherine Motel and am relieved of $150. I remonstrate with the Asian lady behind the desk, telling her that the room I'd booked on my lap top was $90 but, in the end, I go like a lamb to the slaughter as I'm just too hot to argue. As I book in, the Harley rider I'd waved to back at Adelaide River pulls up and we stand by our bikes and chat. Janette is also riding around Australia and agrees to be interviewed. Serendipity strikes again!

Determined to make the most of my $150, I take a dip in the pool, then turn the air conditioning up full blast as I recline on my bed and watch the final of Masterchef! In the morning I drop Percy off to be serviced at the Honda shop, which is handily placed in the same street and chat with Janette outside her motel room in the morning sun.

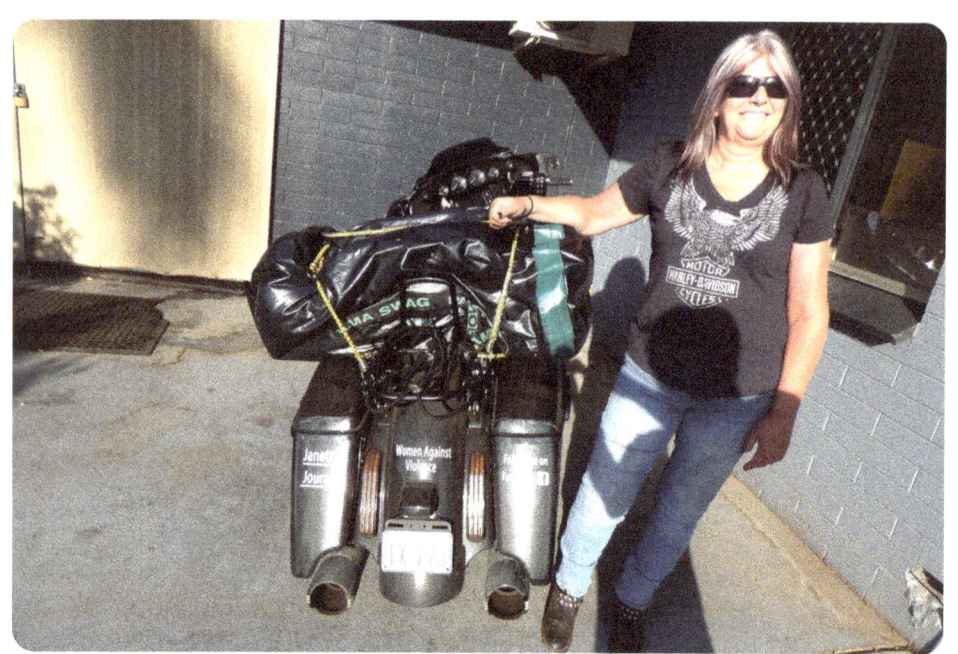

White Ribbon Rider
Janette Mann

Janette draws on her cigarette and blows smoke up and away from me as she answers my first question. "It's simple," she says, "I ride because I love it. I just love the adventure."

Janette rode three quarters of the way around the continent three years previously, shipping her bike to Mackay in Queensland and riding with a group to Darwin, before continuing on her own around the west coast and back to Victoria. This time she wanted the ride to count for something. "There had been lots of murders and attacks on females in Melbourne making the headlines, prior to me leaving on this trip so I thought, what better cause than White Ribbon."

White Ribbon is a not-for-profit organisation that started in Canada in 1991. Its aim is to challenge the outdated, negative concepts of manhood and encourage males to embrace positive change. The white ribbon is symbolically worn by men as a pledge to never commit, condone or remain silent about violence to girls and women.

Galvanised into action, Janette contacted the organisation, registered as a fund raiser, created a 'Give a Little' funding page, twisted the throttle on her Harley Davidson and she was away. She reckons it was surprisingly easy to organise. Leaving work was no problem as she has a very flexible arrangement as a casual Corrections Officer.

"Are there many people doing fund raising trips?" I ask.

"I think so. I crossed paths with a guy riding around for Multiple sclerosis a few weeks ago, going in the other direction."

Janette has had many offers of support and free accommodation since she left her home in Traralgon in Gippsland a couple of months ago and has, she says met some incredible people. "If I were travelling in a car, I know I wouldn't get that response. Riding a bike, especially on your own is so rewarding. You just get so much more."

Janette has no sponsors and says the trip is entirely funded by herself, with all money raised going to the White Ribbon organisation. "It's all about educating the next generation," she says, "in schools and work places. Not just domestic violence but violence of any sort against a woman by a male."

I ask Janette when she learned to ride. "Well I grew up with dirt bikes. Every weekend my dad would pack us three kids and mum in the four-wheel drive and head for the bush. Mum and dad had a bike each and we'd have to wait for our turn to have a go."

Janette's dad set off to ride around the country with two mates, riding a 1940's Indian Chief. He headed south but only got as far as Victoria, where he met Janette's mum. "And that was that," she says, "so part of me is also doing this trip for him. He was the reason I got into bikes I suppose. I spent a lot of time on the back of bikes in my late teens but eventually, after a few false starts I got my full licence."

She didn't venture far on motorcycles though. Before her big trip three years ago, the farthest she'd ridden was 200 kilometres. "Somebody said I couldn't do it and I'm pretty competitive, so it drove me I suppose."

She's a member of the Gippsland and North Melbourne chapters of the HOG (Harley Owners Group) and loves the social aspect of weekend and monthly rides. She says, "they're a great bunch of peo-

ple who also do a lot of fund raising."

I nod towards Janette's bike, which dwarfs my Kawasaki. "Why a Harley?" I ask.

"I just always wanted one. My last trip was on a Yamaha Tracer which did the job but was a bit tall. I was on my tip toes. I'm not getting any younger George, so I just went for comfort. Big motor and a low, comfy seat."

I walk over and sit on Janette's bike, a CVO Street Glide with a monstrous 1923cc motor that is almost three times the size of Percy's. I see what she means; the seat is like an armchair. She wanders over. "I was just saying on my blog the other day though," she says, "that as much as I love the Harley, I think on my next trip I might go for an adventure bike. Maybe a BMW GS 800 so I can go and explore some of the dirt roads."

Janette says writing up her blog, "Janette's Journey" every night can be a pain sometimes but it's worth it as it put the minds of family and friends at ease and puts her in touch with lots of fellow motorcyclists. "I get women telling me that I'm some kind of inspiration," she laughs. "And they say things like, 'I wish I could do that,' and I tell them there's absolutely no reason why you can't. Just get out there and do it!

Chapter Six.

THROUGH THE KIMBERLEY

*"Sun comes up and we all learn.
Those wheels must turn."*

Midnight Oil

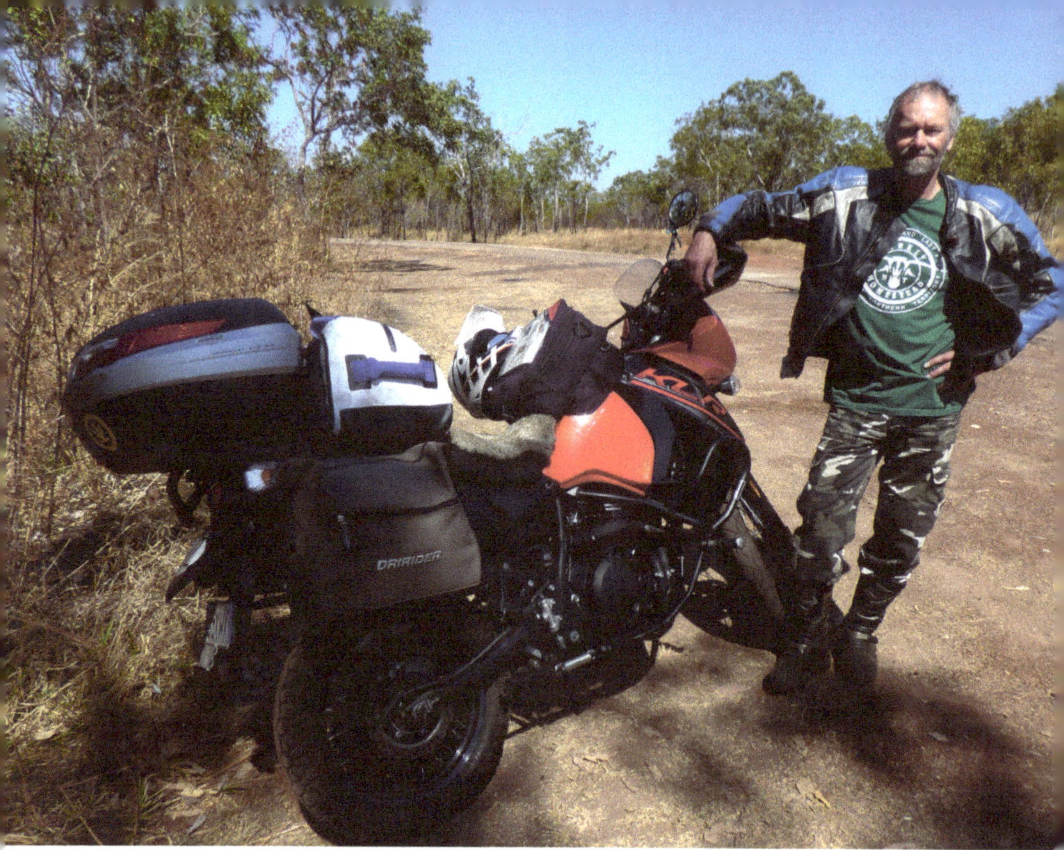
DRIRIDER

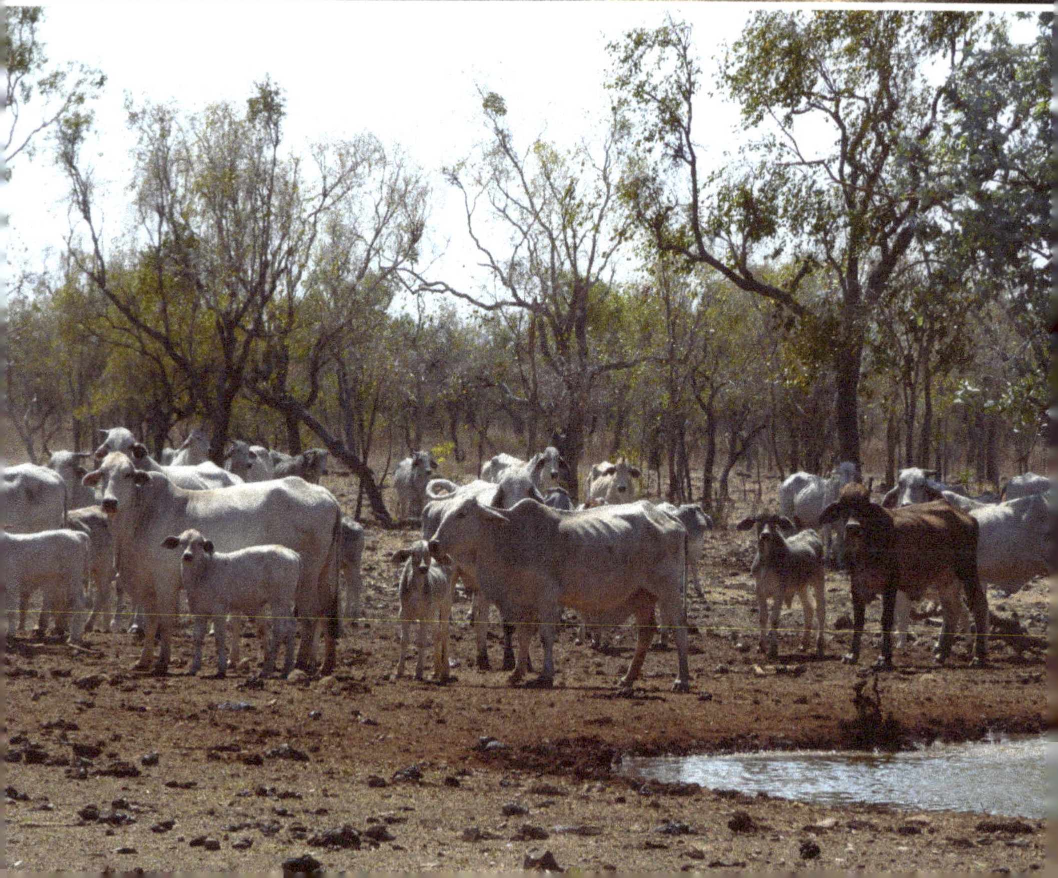

With time on my hands, I wander down to the Katherine River in the growing heat, keeping a weather eye open for crocs. Mayor Fay Miller is apparently in favour of culling. In the Katherine Times she was quoted as saying, "I understand that some people will say we live in their home but they're mixing with civilisation now."

Only the other week the Katherine River's biggest crocodile was captured, sedated and moved to a farm to become part of a live display. The salty, measuring 4.7 metres and weighing in at 600kgs had been hunted for the past ten years. Ranger John Burke, employed by the Parks and Wildlife Commission caught the beast (with a little help) and said, "we moved him to protect people who insist on taking a dip to cool off in the river's largest waterhole."

Wondering why a 'salty' was captured so far from the sea, I wander back through town looking for coffee, passing more Aboriginal people than I've seen in one place before.

Sometimes I read or take notes and sometimes I simply observe,

hopefully in a non-voyeuristic way. I'm doing a bit of both at the moment, sitting in dappled shade at an outdoor picnic table by the information centre taking my morning coffee, that was made in a little caravan. Young mums with toddlers sit on rugs on grass as smooth as a billiard table. One toddler narrowly misses gouging the eye out of another as they sit in the winter sun as two American jet fighters scream over-head, en-route to Darwin. A young hippie-type backpacker sits cross-legged a couple of metres away, a beatific expression on her face as she rolls herself a durry.

    A group of Aboriginal people sit under a tree about 30 metres away and I can't imagine any of them wandering over for a latte. Aboriginal people, (Marie in Darwin told me the term they use amongst themselves is, 'country people' but I don't know if I should use it too. I decide not to) are hard for someone who knows nothing about them to write about. In a town like Katherine, some seem like black ghosts flitting around the periphery of white goings-on, occasionally communicating, but mostly keeping to themselves, dusty, some barefooted and seemingly oblivious to the surroundings. I think we fear them more than they fear us, but our fear comes from a dark well of guilt and hopelessness about how to improve their situation. Am I helping an elderly white-haired man who asks me to "do him a favour" by "lending" him a couple of bucks that I'm pretty sure is going to go on grog? Bill Bryson points out in his excellent book, *Down Under*, "for the first 99.7 per cent of its inhabited history, Aboriginals had Australia to themselves."

Whether through Colonial arrogance, out and out racism or willful ignorance, a huge cultural gulf exists between us. A gulf that hasn't really improved since Captain James Cook tried to make contact with the Dharawal people of Botany Bay almost 250 years ago.

As I clunk freshly-serviced Percy into gear and leave town, I'm thankful that I'm not in a position of power with important decisions to make and can just ride off into the sunset.

The road out of Katherine on the Victoria Highway provides the best riding of the trip so far. The scenery is improving after thousands of kilometres of flatness with red sandstone mesas and the occasional sweeping bend in the road, which my motorcycle serenely banks around. I pass the entrance to the Judbara/Gregory National Park, at 13,000 square kilometres, the second biggest in the NT and whose caves contain an extensive collection of rock art.

The much over-used word 'awesome' best describes the Outback. Humbling is another. I listen to the tyres singing on the tarmac and the regular heartbeat of the KLR's massive single piston. I marvel again at mankind's ability to build something like this motorcycle. A magic carpet which, with minimal effort and maintenance, could

circumnavigate my blue and white planet. My thoughts wander to things I wish I'd done and things I'm proud of, things I'd like to do, things I know I'll never do and embarrassing things I'd like to undo. Annoying things, hopes, dreams and memories. A blurred collage of faces and encounters – a kaleidoscopic journey through my life. Who needs an iPod?

While I take a break in a free camping area, Rupert from Wimbledon in the UK wanders over and asks if I'd like to join him for coffee, an offer I, of course, don't refuse. He and his Aussie wife Sue call Freemantle home and have driven up here in their dusty Landrover Discovery, en route to Darwin where they plan to lend it to their student daughter, till she finishes her studies. "She'll be very popular with her friends!" I say as I enjoy some rare palatable coffee.

As it's a short day at the office, I pull in at the Timber Creek Roadhouse with only 300 k's on the clock. They have a cabin for $70 and as I'm feeling tired, I take it. Later, I bump into White Ribbon Rider Janette in the only bar where she's busy writing her blog. She's frustrated as the Wi-Fi keeps dropping out.

In the morning I sit outside my room with an instant coffee (needs must) and watch the world come to life. Grey Nomads are to-ing and fro-ing to the toilet blocks, while the ever-present pink galahs squawk around them. While I indulge in a croc pie at the café (I've got to say it, "just like chicken") I overhear someone say they've seen a freshwater croc on the other side of the creek. I wander down

and sure enough there he is, prehistoric and magnificent. He looks to be about one and a half metres long, resembling a log and soaking up the sun.

As soon as I cross the border from the Northern Territory into Western Australia, where a young man with a clipboard asks if I have any fruit or vegetables in my panniers, I'm in the Kimberley. This was named after John Wodehouse, 1st Earl of Kimberley and Secretary of State for the Colonies between 1870/74 and 1880/82. This huge region of north-west Australia is largely untouched apart from the fertile river valleys. Its steep limestone and sandstone ridges make many areas inaccessible. The Kimberley is 423,517 square kilometres of rugged wilderness – so huge that you could fit England into it three times!

As I ride, feet up on my highway pegs to give my knees a break, I trawl through old memories and project them up on a big blank screen inside my head. It's at times like these that I'm simply content to be dwelling in the world. The red rocky outcrops and dry yellow grass take me back to 1984 and the Hwange National Park in Zimbabwe. Adrift in reverie, memories wash over me.

I'd had only been in Africa for a couple of weeks and was travelling with a couple of Welsh guys. The Zimbabwean Game Warden, khaki-clad and slightly chubby, had driven us from camp into the wilds and had parked his Landrover under a tree about an hour before.

"Well, a pride of lion was spotted here earlier," he says, indicating the map he'd spread on the bonnet, "shall we try to spot them on foot?"

We agree in unison and are soon marching purposefully over the baked-earth, through the acacia trees and thorn bushes. We walk for another half-hour or so and it suddenly dawns on me that I'm not reading a Wilbur Smith novel but am actually walking through the African bush for God's sake! A little quiver of excitement courses up my spine after this reality check, and I make sure I'm not too far away from our warden and his FN rifle. Suddenly he freezes and we almost clatter into him. He motions us (unnecessarily) to halt and points up a faint game trail through the tall yellow grass.

We all crouch down like they do in war movies and a long tawny body crosses over about fifty yards ahead. A lioness! Two small cubs follow, and we spot more bodies ahead. Silently the Warden motions us to follow him and we take a wide arc to our left. The adrenaline starts to pump as we tiptoe in a half-crouch behind our man and I heard Wynn say, "shit!" under his breath. I hope like hell that we don't surprise one of them.

The Warden has now spotted clear paw prints in the sand and we follow cautiously, treading on eggs shells. We come to a halt and in a whisper, we're warned of the dangers of lions with cubs to protect. "Do you want to go closer?"

We all nod, and it might have been my imagination, but Gill and Wynn's eyes are like saucers. No doubt, mine are too. We continue for another ten minutes in this vein, hoping we're out of sight, when rounding a bend in the trail we spot them. I hear a low rumbling belly cough, "A warning," says the Warden as calm as-you-like, "they know we are here," as he cocks his rifle. The noise of the bolt sounds like an explosion in the silence. The lions are gathered in a clearing less than a hundred yards off, two males, six lionesses and some cubs.

"Closer?" whispers the warden. You must be having a laugh, I think, but simply nod. I certainly do not want to go any closer, but there you go. Gill catches my eye with his eyebrows raised to his forehead and his eyes now the size of dinner plates. "If there is big trouble you must each find a tree and run and climb it," says the warden.

I wonder about his definition of 'big trouble' and worse still, realise that the largest 'tree' around is only a bush that comes up to my navel. In fact, being totally honest with myself, I realise that my legs are not about to take me anywhere in their present jelly-like condition.

I try to swallow and discover that my throat's as dry as an ashtray. The pride has now made its way up the rocky hillside, some cubs scampering to the top and a couple in the mouths of lionesses. The smaller male with an undeveloped mane follows, leaving the big one to cover their retreat. Why on earth they feel they have to retreat from us is beyond me.

Foolishly, Gill and Wynn move closer, cameras poised. The Warden tut-tuts and brings his rifle up to his shoulder. We must have overstepped some invisible boundary because suddenly, the large male lion loses his temper and in a fluid motion, rushes towards us, his ears flat and his belly close to the ground. I look about frantically, sphincter tightening. Oh fuck! We all retreat hastily, walking backwards, me making sure I stay right behind the bloke with the gun.

About twenty or so yards away, (though it is only later I can think rationally) the great beast stops with a snarl, in a cloud of dust, tail lashing. I look into those eyes like hot coals, and all I see is hate and complete disdain for puny Homo sapiens. The warden covers our retreat as, grinning idiotically, we congratulate one another on our photography. The lion turns with royal disdain, his job done – the puny intruders put in their place. He turns his huge head one more time as he heads up the hill to his waiting pride.

Back in Australia, I'm soon in Kununurra, a pleasant, if uninspiring service town, riding around in the 30-degree heat, looking for some shade and a decent coffee, a rare thing let me tell you. I venture into the Kununurra Hotel for liquid solace, but the place has a dark and brooding ambience that's depressing. The place smells of decades of cigarette smoke and spilt beer, the TV screens blare horse racing and suspicious looks from the three or four serious drinkers don't entice me to stay. I make do with a mango smoothie in a pleasant café nearby and put my watch back an hour and a half as I slurp.

I cross over the brown waters of the Ord River, controversially dammed in 1971 for irrigation and responsible for the creation of Lake Argyle, the second-largest man-made lake on the continent. Its average surface area is 1,000 square kilometres and is home to 25,000 freshwater crocs. The Hydro plant provides power to Kununurra, Wyndham and the Argyle Diamond Mine, which along with the Ellendale Mine nearby, provides a third of the world's diamonds.

An hour later, and now heading south on the Great Northern Highway, I pull into the Doon Doon Roadhouse. I could camp here but it's a still a bit early (and no Wi-fi) so I have a cuppa tea (coffee's only instant) and press on as I see there's another roadhouse an hour down the road. Percy takes a good ten minutes to get started, backfiring and causing some blackbirds to take flight, which is very frustrating.

Baob trees, with their distinctive bottle-shaped trunks, are numerous here, adding to the impression of Africa. They can grow up to 15 metres in height but are smaller than their African cousins known as baobab trees. It's not uncommon for baobabs to live for over 2,000 years and measure over 15 metres in circumference. A large hollowed-out baob tree in Derby, a couple of day's ride ahead is said to have been used in the 1890s as a lock-up for Aboriginal prisoners en route to jail and is now a tourist attraction.

Riding 100 k's here is nothing like riding 100 k's in New Zealand where the roads are narrower and twistier. The speed limit is 110 kph and you know that, in an hour's time, you'll have done over 100 kilometres! There are some big sweeping bends, curling around some low red hills. Some of the bridges are very long, testament to the flooding that takes place during the big wet (November to April) when 90% of the annual rainfall drenches the land. It's August now and most bridges span dry red earth. It's the perfect time to travel

the north – no rain, no mossies, not many flies and a constant maximum of around 30 degrees.

My single cylinder 649cc motor drones along and I play mental games to keep alert. I see how many US presidents I can name, getting back only as far as Roosevelt and World War 11, then try to sing every lyric to a whole album. Today I choose one of my all-time favourites – Bowie's 1974 dystopian masterpiece, *Diamond Dogs*, but get stuck trying to sing *Chant of the Ever Circling Skeletal Family*. I drive my kids mad when I tell them (only when asked) how much I hate modern R&B and rap. Instead of it being "edgy" I just find it tame, soulless and all a bit sad.

Just before the Turkey Creek Roadhouse I pass a bright orange clad postman on a postie bike doing a U-turn and try to imagine how big his route must be! As I book a spot for my tent, a grey-bearded, red-faced Yorkshireman asks the guy behind the counter for some chain lube and I realise that I'd mistaken him for the postman! 74-year-old Richard is touring the Kimberley on a 110cc postie bike and soon has his tent pitched next to mine. I lube his chain for him and he regales me with his travel tales for the rest of night. He wants to buy me a cold beer but inside, we're told that the Aboriginal Warmun Community is a dry one and so have to settle for chocolate milk. At least it's cold. These "dry" regions are excellent ideas as let's face it, most of the modern problems relating to Aboriginal Communities are caused by the demon drink. The young guy serving me tells us that alcohol restrictions have helped to dramatically decrease the number of assaults and drink driving arrests recently.

Postie Bike Rider
Richard Wilkinson

"So, Richard," I start our little chat and sip my chocolate milk, "what are you doing on a postie bike in the middle of the Kimberley?"

"Well, I worked in the Kimberley as a young man in the early '60s and never did the 'tourist thing', as I was saving money for a trip to Canada. So, here I am."

He freighted his little bike to Kununurra from his home in Perth and has ridden it to Lake Argyle and Wyndham and plans to continue to Broome. "I did fancy doing the Gibb River Road but realised that I was probably too old for all those corrugations at 74. My body as had a few prangs and it's pretty buggered now." I tell Richard that my idea of "buggered" is an old bloke in a nursing home, sitting on a lazy-boy with a beer, watching sport, not touring on a little bike and camping out. "Oh no," he shakes his head, "that's a no, no!"

"I've kind of done it tough in life really," he says, "I'm dyslexic and have never had any education or anything. It's been a battle, but I think I've done OK, all things considered."

I ask him to start at the beginning and he's happy to oblige.

"I was born on the Yorkshire Dales and had a rough trot as a child. I was abused and all that sort of crap. When I was 17, I started working for this farmer who was as hard-as-nails but a fair man – a typical Yorkshireman. I told him I wanted adult wages and he told me he'd pay it if I was worth it – and he did."

It was a turning point for Richard, from being put down all his life, to gaining a degree of self-confidence for the first time. After a year of hard graft, the farmer suggested that young Richard go to Australia to satisfy his wanderlust. "I applied to emigrate – you know, a '10-pound tourist' but was knocked back because of an accident I'd had earlier, where a tractor had rolled on me," Richard says.

So, he paid his own fair and arrived in Sydney in 1964. Determined to work in the bush Richard landed a job as a drover's cook. "Cookie Wilkinson!" I say.

"Fantastic job," he laughs, "we brought a mob of sheep down from Blackhall in Queensland to Parkes in NSW. I drove the truck and cooked, and every night I'd put up this fence to keep the sheep in. I made billy-tea and damper, and we'd eat a sheep a week. I'd shoot emus for dog food and the drover told me not to let the Duke of Edinburgh know as they were protected."

Richard then worked as a train drover, looking after sheep that were sent by rail from Bourke to Sydney before being shipped to Mexico. "So, I thought, aha! Here's my opportunity to travel to Mexico," he says. "I travelled with 17,000 sheep to Manzanu in Mexico on the Panamanian registered, SS Eros, a single-screwed, four-cylinder steamship with a mostly Fijian crew."

In Fiji and then Tahiti the crew went on strike because they hadn't been paid and later 1200 sheep had to be thrown into the sea to create extra room for ventilation for the remaining sheep. "We were very popular with the sharks!" says Richard. More strife followed in Mexico when the (still unpaid) crew threatened to mutiny. When the crew threatened to kill the Chief Engineer, Richard and the 1st Mate were tasked with getting him off the ship to safety.

"None of us were being paid so we stole things off the ship to sell onshore. I was elected salesman and my job was to sell some sheep that we'd held back when most of them were offloaded. We sent them down in a bosun's chair and gave the Customs people a sheep as a backhander. I sold them all over town, even to the brothels. Picture a 20-year-old virgin selling Australian sheep to a Mexican brothel!"

After nursing the SS Eros back to Sydney, Richard had a stint at fruit picking before sailing to New Zealand, where he assembled woodworking machines in Auckland for a year. Richards attributes his "social disease" which I assume is his lack of confidence as the reason for his nomadic tendencies and reckons the only way he found to combat it, was to constantly be on the move. Returning by boat to the UK, he became a stonemason, working for a while on the new network of Motorways.

After a camping trip to Russia, where he almost caused a political incident on the Polish border, Richard headed to South Africa, working his passage on a ship loaded with cattle. "I was officially an Agricultural Worker," he explains, "I looked after the cattle and was invited onto the properties in South Africa by the owners. It was great, and I was asked to stay but the apartheid business put me off."

He then sailed to Western Australia and arrived in Freemantle with $15 in his pocket. "I travelled up here to the Kimberley and worked for a year before travelling on to Canada."

Richard, as you'd imagine had many adventures on his way to Canada. After hitching across Australia to Sydney, he worked his passage on a ship to Panama and after teaming up with a Kiwi guy, spent the next six months travelling up to the American border. "We then bought a car and drove up the west side of the USA into Canada and I ended up working on the southern tip of Hudson Bay."

Richard's nomadic life continued with him returning to the UK and getting married. "We went back to Australia, but my English wife found it not to her liking, so we compromised and went to New Zealand," he says. After living in Waikouaiti, near Dunedin for a spell, Richard persuaded his wife to return to Western Australia where they had a son and have lived ever since, with Richard working mainly as a carpenter, all over the state, and occasionally heading off on solo adventures.

"Twelve years ago," Richard says, "I was diagnosed with Alzheimer's Disease. I read up about it. If I get too stressed it can be difficult. I lost it in Buenos Aires about five years ago when I was on the way to Cuba, but some Americans were very kind and helped me out."

I tell him there doesn't seem to be much wrong with his memory, as he lists all the countries he's visited in the last decade, of which there are many. "I can remember back then, it's what happened five minutes ago that's the problem," he explains. "It's good for me to be on Betsy, my postie bike, with all my little bits of kit. You have to exercise the old brain. But I still lose things. In Kunanurra I lost my keys and was convinced I'd left them in the shower. I even reported them missing in the office, then I found them in my pocket!" and he laughs.

As with many of the people I meet on my travels, Richard deserves a whole book or at least a whole chapter on his colourful, adventurous life. He entertains me with tales of enduro racing, encounters with lions, black bears and officialdom that make my hair curl.

Always on a budget, Richard's most recent adventures include walking the Kokoda Track, whose 96 kilometres through the incredibly rugged Owen Stanley Range in Papua New Guinea, took him ten days. "Cruel walking. Punishing on the knees but by God those locals are tough!" He also travelled to Antarctica and Greenland, "just to have a look."

Back in Perth, Richard lives in a big shed out the back, while his wife has the house. "It's a great arrangement," he says, "we're still friends but she's not as rough and ready as me."

He still works and has a small gardening business, as well as making coffins as a side-line, "only mine has built-in wine racks!"

There's nothing like travel to give you self-confidence and a feeling of self-worth, George," he says, and I nod in agreement.

Nature calls in the middle of the night (I knew I shouldn't have had that last chocolate milk) and I must get up for the inevitable pee. I look up, mesmerised by the splendour of the night sky. With no clouds and zero light pollution, the stars burn sharply. I note a particularly bright one and wonder if it's the Humanity Star, launched last year from New Zealand by Rocket Lab founder Peter Beck. The controversial sphere is, in fact, a carbon-fibre disco ball, one metre in diameter. With its 65 highly reflective panels, it spins rapidly and is visible from anywhere on Earth at certain times. Visionary Peter Beck's idea, is to draw our gaze up to the heavens in an effort to get us to look beyond our day-to-day concerns, and try to consider the big-picture. Its nine-month orbit is almost over, and the eight kg disco ball is set to burn up in the atmosphere any day. Beck plans to launch more Humanity Stars in the future and I take my hat off to him. I also notice that back on Earth, I've splashed a bit of wee on my bare foot.

In the cool of the morning, Richard the Postie Bike Man recedes in Percy's mirrors with a cheery wave and soon becomes a dot, an inspirational character it was my pleasure to meet. Under another cloudless sky, I enjoy a couple more hours of glorious riding before pulling into Halls Creek.

Europeans came here in the late 19th century looking for pasture for their sheep and cattle but of course, the land had been known and occupied for many thousands of years before that. The ancient land is crisscrossed with trading paths and song lines. Sitting on the

northern edge of the Great Sandy Desert and the only town in 600 kms of the Great Northern Highway, Halls Creek is another small service town with communities of Gooniyandi, Jaru and Kija people. It provides a good reason to stretch my legs and 'youbeuady!', the Information Centre has Wi-fi and passable coffee.

Many Aboriginal people wander about, mixing with the tourists. In fact, indigenous people represent 70% of the town's population. The men seem to be slight, some sporting Acubra hats, checked shirts and cowboy boots, while the women are stouter. All have incredibly thin legs. I find them fascinating and try not to stare. Attempts to engage a couple of them in conversation lead to varying results. Some laugh, some ignore me. To be honest I'm a bit embarrassed at my wariness when I'm in their presence and embarrassed too at my ignorance.

Almost 300 kilometres of bush then flashes by as if in a trance. My world is the road, the bush and the sky, like a blue blanket. I travel on the centre line for tens of k's at a time till oncoming traffic forces me back to my lane. The roadkill has changed recently from mostly grey and red 'roos farther east to wild black pigs and cattle. A wedge-tailed eagle soars above me and I try and imagine the fabulous view from up there.

I finally fetch-up at the Fitzroy Crossing River Lodge and just as I'm pitching my tent I'm joined by three bikers who do the same. Actually, they have swags, which are basically sleeping bags, inside a waterproof outer with a built-in groundsheet. Their only drawback is that there's no room for your gear. Over a few schooners and goat curry at the busy Lodge, we swap tales. Their bikes of choice are, a new MV Augusta (an interesting choice), a Triumph Tiger and a venerable BMW GS 1200 Adventure and they're doing half a lap, having ridden up from Melbourne through the centre and turned left at Katherine. Two of them are retired Motorcycle cops from the Isle of Man, so they naturally have a few yarns up their sleeve. I love camping as it affords me the opportunity to have a chat, especially when the old amber liquid is around to settle the dust and loosen tongues. The camaraderie between motorcyclists is sometimes quite special and this is one of those occasions.

Many of the businesses in Fitzroy Crossing are run by Aboriginal Communities. As a town it hasn't a great deal to recommend it apart from being the centre of many tourist destinations such as the Geike Gorge, where the Fitzroy River has carved the limestone to create an amazing formation 60 metres high and 14 kilometres long. My new friends are obviously not as concerned with the wildlife threat as I am, as they leave at first light, while I'm still half asleep. The way-too-loud, crackling exhaust of the MV Augusta would have done nothing to further relations between motorcyclists and grey nomads I'm sure!

The next 169 kms on a dead-straight road are a bit of a slog and when a stopping place appears, I pull off and sit at a table in the shade. I love the quiet. It's natural. For almost all of our couple of million years of existence, our genus Homo have lived our lives surrounded by the quiet of nature. Later I have a proper stop and a coffee, which I can only describe as 'intriguing,' from a machine at the Willare Bridge Roadhouse. These roadhouses present a most welcome oasis in a sea of wilderness and draw travellers like magnets. They seem to be manned by mostly backpackers needing cash, who work there for three-month stretches before moving on.

Chapter Seven.

HEADING SOUTH

*"There's so much left to know and
I'm on the road to find out."*

Cat Stevens.

Stinger Relief Station

LIONS CLUB OF BROOME

Stinger Relief Station

Vinegar

T he YHA hostel in central Broome is amazing. It's more like a resort, with pool, bar and non-stop R&B music blaring out of speakers. I feel a bit long-in-the-tooth, surrounded as I am by young, cool, tanned, exhibitionist, smoking backpackers.

I soon discover that Broome, named after the WA Governor Sir Frederick Broome (1883 – 1889) is not walker-friendly. Like most towns around here, it's very spaced out, with no real centre, unless you count Maccers, KFC, Dominos Pizza and a Police Station as the Town Centre. The beaches are amazing though, full of beautiful, tanned young-things, throwing frisbees, swigging beer, smoking and playing with their phones. Oh, to be young again! I ride Percy out to the 22 km long Cable beach, six k's out of town and so named because it's here the Australia-Java undersea cable comes ashore.

I lay in the top bunk, tossing and turning till the music finally stops around midnight. It's your own fault! I tell myself. Percy decides to start first pop in the morning, and I leave town early as I've a long ride ahead. Feeling the reassuring vibration of the big single cylinder through the tank, I head south, bidding adieu to the awesome Kimberley. I may have broken my own golden rule because a few 'roos are still grazing by the roadside, but thankfully bounce away, into the bush. The red kangaroo, along with the crocodile are two examples of ancient Australian megafauna that are happily still with us. Scientist believe that the extinction of Australian megafauna such as the marsupial lion, giant kangaroo and diprotodon was probably the first significant mark Homo Sapiens made on planet Earth. The diprotodon was the largest marsupial to have ever lived and resembled a hippopotamus sized wombat. According to Wikipedia, it's claimed that Aboriginal rock paintings in traditional Quinkan country in Queensland depict these giants. In fact, Australia boasts the dubious distinction of having the world's highest mammal extinction rate with more than 10% of natives wiped out in the last two centuries. Since Cook visited in 1770, 34 mammals and 29 birds have gone, never to return. Many more native species are at risk, especially in the Northern Territories.

By the time I've ridden the 286 kilometres of long, straight highway to the Sandfire Roadhouse, I'm more than ready for a break. On my left is the Great Sandy Desert, and on my right the Indian Ocean. The map on my tank bag is superfluous – in fact, the area it shows

today has more white nothingness than any since I left Sydney. It's no wonder then that the wind is often ferocious with nothing to impede its progress. At times I'm crouched over my tank with the peak of my helmet almost touching the top of my screen.

At the Roadhouse, I sit outside with a passable coffee and an egg sandwich as a peacock's trumpet frightens the life out of some Chinese tourists. It's here I meet retired couple, Cheryl and Chris from Tasmania who are on a four-month trip around the country. They are engaged in a worldwide phenomenon called Geocaching, which they explain, is a form of treasure hunting. It's a recreational activity in which participants use a GPS to find small hidden containers. Inside is a logbook which you sign with your personal code name and date before returning it to the same spot. "Come with me," says Cheryl commandingly and I follow them behind the Roadhouse to an old fridge. "Voila!" says Chris and under the fridge is a small Tupperware container with some paper and a pen. "You're what's known as a 'muggle'" says Cheryl, "as in, someone who travels around but doesn't play."

Leaving them to their Geocaching (which sounds quite cool and fair play to them) I muggle on down the road, catching glimpses of the sand dunes of Eighty Mile Beach to my right and then pass the turn-off to the Nyangumarta Highway to my left. This is a red dirt road, who's restricted access brings you, after 600 kilometres onto

the famous Canning Stock Route. This ride is for serious adventurers only. Its 1850 rugged kilometres take you across the Great Sandy Desert and I kid myself that I'm going to ride it one day with my mate 'Mad Max' O'Brien. I've a feeling that life will get in the way. It's mustering time on the Stations hereabouts, as pastoralists prepare to send their cattle to Port Hedland. Over 5,000 are expected to be sent to Indonesia in the next two months as live exports.

Port Hedland, not miss-spelt but named after a Captain Hedland who anchored his ship here in 1863, is one of the world's busiest and

largest harbour. It transports millions of tons of raw materials (90% iron ore) and live cattle all over the planet. It's great to watch the monstrous machinery in action, and it's all on display here. But like most towns hereabouts, it's just too spread out to be walkable and has no real centre. I finally pitch my tent at the Blackrock campsite and meet accountant Mike from Brisbane who's riding his BMW GS 800 on a 'full lap of the paddock'. He had no experience on a motorcycle before deciding to swap the office for the open road and prefers to ride dirt roads wherever possible. Tiring of cold, thrown-together dinners, I walk the three k's to the nearest restaurant and treat myself to fish 'n' chips and salad. In the morning Mike helps me to bump start Percy and later, overtakes me with a wave.

The day offers up more, dead-straight road that disappears over the rim of the planet, bisecting parched red earth and spinifex scrub under the relentless sun. Outside of my hypnotic bike-in-motion universe I know there are babies being born, old people taking their last breath, cattle dying of thirst and young couples sharing a first kiss. Storms, wars and earthquakes, terror and joy and all the machinations of a seven billion strong anthill. On roads as flat and featureless as this, the bike kind of runs itself and I can drift away on a sea of reminiscence, though a small percentage of my grey matter

controls my peripheral vision and is constantly on yellow alert for the danger of wildlife.

I glance at Mr. Spock, cable-tied to my right mirror with his hand splayed in the Vulcan greeting, "Live long and prosper." I've been obsessed with Star Trek since it first appeared on British screens as syndicated reruns in the early '70s and it's fair to say that it changed my life. In fact, I'd go as far as to say that it helped change the world. The hairs on my young neck would stand up as William Shatner's voice intoned, "Space. The final frontier. These are the voyages of the Starship Enterprise …" And I'd be spellbound for the next hour as the intrepid crew boldly went where no *one* has gone before. (Twenty years later the more cerebral and enlightened Captain Picard and his crew went where no one had gone before) At the time, the Vietnam War was still going strong, the Cold War was at its height and Britain was suffering recession, industrial action and power cuts. For my young and impressionable mind, Star Trek represented the only positive view of the future. Creator Gene Roddenberry was a visionary, who imagined a future where the United Federation of Planets explored the galaxy, without racism or bigotry, but still featured short skirts and fistfights. It was social commentary disguised as Science Fiction. I still love those original 79 episodes today and can recite the scripts almost word for word. I'm still amazed at what they achieved on such a low budget. Call me an old fart, but I don't care for the new movies. Roddenberry's ideals have been hijacked. The complex, symbiotic relationship between Kirk, Spock and McCoy that formed the bedrock of the show has been replaced by wise-cracking and cartoonish actors cavorting about the galaxy like a *Fast and Furious* movie.

Kirk and Spock became my mentors, (the old man was 'missing in action' on that front) along with Muhammad Ali, David Carradine's character Kwai Chan Caine from the TV show Kung Fu, Bob Dylan and David Bowie. Sick puppy eh?

Now on the Coastal Highway, though I can't actually see the coast, I enter the Pilbara region. I take my coffee at the Whim Creek Hotel, a great spot with free camping that's tailor-made for chance encounters with Crocodile Dundee-like characters but alas, not today. In the late 1800s copper and gold were discovered nearby and today the Hotel's facilities are used by the workers from the Whim Creek Copper Mine. The big bearded barman warns me of the wind. "Could blow a sailor off ya sister!" he says, snickering at his own joke, and waving, "Seeyuzlader!"

Back in the saddle, the wind gusts are outrageous. The jury is out on whether it's better to lean into the wind or, as some suggest, lean away and create a wedge for the wind to pass over, which is counter-intuitive. I just go by my gut feeling and try not to overthink it. At one point I'm blown clear across the highway but fortunately, there's nothing coming the other way. After that, I slow down to around 80 kph when I see a road train approaching, just in case. Taking a break in the shade at a 24-hour stopping place, I listen to a toddler screaming a temper-tantrum from the back of a Land Cruiser. "Got room on the back of your bike for a three-year-old?" the mum asks me. "No thanks. Been there and done that!" I reply with a smile.

Roebourne is the oldest surviving town on the north-west coast, dating from 1864. It's here I turn off and ride the 12 kilometres to tiny Cossack on the coast, where my friend of a friend and contact Tiffany is helping to organise an Aboriginal art exhibition, part of the Cossack Art Awards. It's still as windy as hell, a thing that people are strangely apologetic about, along with the cold snap. It's only

25 degrees! Cossack is popular with tourists and boasts National Trust listed blue stone buildings from the late 1800s and it's in one of these that I meet Tiffany. She's promised to find an interesting character for me to interview in Karratha where she lives, and where I plan to stay for a few days.

The Karratha Backpackers has a very relaxed feel about it, due in no small measure to dreadlocked and laid-back owner Terry 'Gonzo' Flanagan. He has that peaceful, Zen-like air of having seen it all and isn't about to be shocked by anything else. The Hostel is full of young travellers from overseas, most of them working or looking for work. Apparently, to qualify for another year on a working holiday visa, they must work for a minimum of 88 days in the 'regions'.
A stunning-looking girl in her early 20's from California explains this to me as she chain-smokes. She acts as though she were in a Hollywood 'B' Movie and her sentences are laced with swear words that would make a sailor blush. An American guy mumbles, "potty mouth," to her as he passes by. An enthusiastic young English guy with a green KLR 650 is putting new tyres on his bike in the courtyard and I lend him my tools and what I hope is some sage advice. I drop Percy at the Honda shop in the industrial area for a new rear tyre and hitch back to the Hostel.

When I pick the bike up next morning the owner says the valves are fine, but he's put in a new spark plug in an attempt to fix the starting problem. It seems to have worked and I ride to nearby Dampier, established in the1960's by Hamersley Iron and home of the famous Red Dog.

Also known as Bluey and Tally Ho, Red Dog was a kelpie, famous for his travels throughout Western Australia in the 1970s. He had a series of owners but also travelled on his own, becoming something of a mascot for the Pilbara community. He was apparently a member of the local union and had his own bank account with the Bank of New South Wales, who used him in advertising logos. He was deliberately poisoned with strychnine in 1979 and buried in an unmarked grave in Roebourne by vet Rick Fenny. I well remember the movie *Red Dog*, based on the clever canine's life, which came out in 2011. At movie's end, my wife, two kids and I were all blubbering in unison in row 'C' as we thought of our family pet Maisy who is a kelpie and a dead ringer for Red Dog.

Next day I hook up with Tiffany, who's working at the impressive Red Earth Arts Precinct. She kindly gives me a tour of the area in her SUV with running commentary, before dropping me off at the house of a real character who, she says is eager to share his story.

'The Sarge'

The Sarge, big and imposing, with a grey beard and ruddy complexion, started working for Rio Tinto in 1971 in Paraburdoo a year before it was officially gazetted as a town. Paraburdoo is an Aboriginal word meaning 'white cockatoo.'

"It was a pretty town. I worked on 'the hill', lubricating or greasing the big trucks for a year," he says. The tipper trucks he worked on were 75 tonners, which were babies he says compared to today's 200 tonne monsters. "In the '70s Hamersley Iron, a subsidiary company of Rio Tinto never sacked anyone, they just transferred them. I was transferred here to Karratha to this street of brand-spanking-new houses and bought this house later with the company's HOP, or Home Ownership Purchases scheme. And I've lived here ever since. I retired in 2014."

I suggest that he must have seen some changes. "All that out there," he says gesturing to the sports complex across the road, "used to be mud, salt flats and mangrove. Karratha means 'soft earth' and all this land was crabhole country. They brought in millions of tons of sand and just built on top of it."

He sips his coke before continuing, "There were so many funny characters. I worked on the front line, loading ships out at Parker Point. The trains are made up of three locomotives pulling 240 wagons, each containing 120 tonnes of iron ore."

I ask him about the process. "It's pretty straightforward," he says, "they drill into a hill, blast it, crush it up and ship it out. They crush it to about 6mm, called lump ore and crush it up into sand which is called fines. But there's obviously more to it than that. There's high-grade and low-grade ore from various Rio mines and what they do is blend it so that it's 76% iron ore when it goes out."

Things have progressed over the decades, from working with shovels (banjos) to today where it's fully automated. Apparently, the control centre in Perth, called The Rock, controls all the machinery via satellite. "They've even got the trains running on their own. There won't be any jobs for the workers soon," he says matter-of-factly.

Sarge looks across the sports field, sips his can of coke (I've got tea) and talks about the good old days. "There was none of this Hi-Viz stuff. None of that. We worked in T-shirt and shorts. You could take your shirt off, but you'd come out black as the ace of spades

with all the iron ore. As long as you wore your boots and helmet you were right. Back in the day, 'dozers didn't have air conditioning so it could get bloody hot! Back then most of it went to Japan and Europe. We had the pellet plant which kept us busy." The pellet plant produced perfectly spherical balls of iron, which Sarge says, didn't come cheap. The raw ore was crushed up with a paste, then put through a balling mill, before going into the furnace. In 1990 Sarge was one of a party sent to Japan to see for themselves what became of the iron ore. "It was a sort of goodwill gesture from the company, as they were having Union problems," he says. "It took us about 16 hours to load a ship and it took the Japanese the same amount of time to unload them. They were very efficient." Back then in the 70's, it was a 20-day turn-around to Japan and often, as many as 14 ships were anchored and waiting, "a whole fleet of 'em sitting out there," he says gesturing out to sea.

I ask him how the ships have changed over the years. "Huge!" he replies, "The ships we used to load were around 120,000 tons, but these days they're more like 260,000 tonnes. The Chinese ones are monsters – seven or eight stories up from the deck or about 70 metres up from the waterline. But they only have a crew of 22," he shrugs. A sign of the times.

I sense a fair degree of bitterness when the Sarge talks about Rio Tinto, though he reckons that working for them in the early days was very good. "I refer to them as a 'bully company'" he says. "When the boom ended seven or eight years ago, they did the dirty on a lot of people. They shut so much down and got rid of so many people, like that," and he clicks his fingers. "A lot of people went through a lot of hardship. Some lost their houses, some even committed suicide. In Karratha today, there are so many empty houses with nobody to rent them."

Nowadays, Sarge says mine employees work on the "FIFO" method, or "Fly in Fly out". They fly in and work for two weeks, then fly home for a week. Workers live in quarters on site, working twelve-hour shifts. This system, according to him has been the ruination of mining towns in the north-west and the reason for their decline, as workers have no investment in the towns.

"What FIFO really means," he says, "is, 'fit in or fuck off'. They're as cunning as shit-house rats! With Hammersly Iron we had job security. These days there's a climate of fear. You have to keep your opinions to yourself or you'll get a black mark and the next time there're cuts, you're down the road. I've heard workers tell me they've had meetings with Human Resources where the first question put them is, 'tell me why we shouldn't terminate you?' I could go on George. What the Unions fought for all those years is gone. Today you're just a number. You're not Joe Bloggs or Joe Blow, you're just a number."

Lightening the tone a bit I ask Sarge if he was around when Red Dog was roaming the Pilbara. "Oh yeah," he says, "he was a real character. I used to ride on the bus with him. He was a stinking dog; never had a bath. And if you sat in his seat-look out! If you sat next to him, he'd growl at you till you moved. He was a pain in the arse. If a truck driver left his door open, he'd be in there and you couldn't get him out!"

I spend the next couple of days catching up on some writing in the excellent library, getting a haircut and just chilling out at the hostel, being entertained by a diverse cast of characters. I wander around in the sun and discover that ten percent of the 16,000 population are Aboriginal and Torres Strait Islanders and the isolated town provides accommodation for the workforce from the offshore North West Shelf petrol and gas venture.

Tiffany suggests that I visit Roebourne again where she says tourists can watch artists at work. On my third ride north to Roebourne, 40 kilometres up the road I finally manage to find someone at home at Yinjaa-Barni Art, located in a Heritage-listed cottage on the main road. A sign outside says that visitors are welcome, so I go in. It's empty apart from Justina, who smilingly allows me to look around at artworks, some hanging, some stacked on the tables and on the ground. "The Aunties aren't here yet, but they'll be here soon painting," she says, "it's quiet now but it can get noisy once the grandchildren are running around." Long tables full of paint, canvas and brushes speak of the hive of activity to come. Justina is very helpful and allows me to take photos.

Yinjaa-Barni Art is a non-profit Aboriginal corporation governed by its own Aboriginal board. Its group of artists predominantly belong to the Yindjibarndi-language group, whose ancestral home is around the Millstream/Tablelands area of the Pilbara. Yinjaa-Barni means "staying together" in the Yindibarndi language. Justina tells

me that she and her family spend time 'out bush' every weekend in the nearby Millstream National Park, being inspired by the beauty of their surroundings. Many of the artworks painted here have won regional and international competitions, been shown in national and international galleries and can be found in private and public collections nationally and internationally. I fall in love with one of Justina's paintings and say I'll buy it if she poses with it, which she reluctantly does. I picture the painting proudly hanging on my office wall in Christchurch. After Justina rolls up the canvas in bubble wrap, I reverently place it in my top box and when I leave Karratha next morning and head south, I'm a happy man.

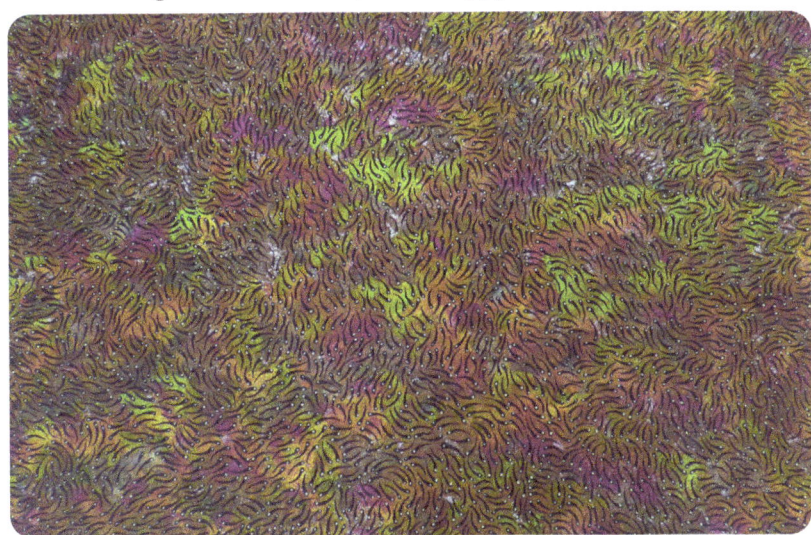

Back on the North West Coastal Highway, time is only defined by the gradual movement of my old-fashioned odometer and the low, old-fashioned stone markers that count down every ten kilometres to the next town or roadhouse. I occasionally pull off the road onto the red dirt and stretch my legs. I've only got to walk 30 metres into the bush to feel like I'm the only person on Earth.

Enjoying my eggs and bacon at the Fortescue River Roadhouse, a Kiwi sheep shearer from Omakau stops at my table and introduces himself as Barry. As I chew, I get his truncated life story. "What about them Crusaders last night eh?" I shake my head and shrug as my mouth is full. "As long as the AB's beat the Aussies, I don't give a fuck. Keep it safe mate!" he says and exits stage-left. I sip my coffee and read that today, Australia's population officially hit 25 million, of which 67% are concentrated around the coast and two-fifths call Sydney and Melbourne home. There's definitely a distribution problem and the Government are understandably keen for new arrivals to find other places to live.

The next 160 kilometres of riding to the Nanutarra Roadhouse is a bit of a struggle as once again the wind is terrific with gusts hitting me like hammer blows. I almost come to a complete halt a couple of times to inch around some brown cattle that are standing, unconcerned, on the highway. I pass over the Tropic of Capricorn once more and as though I've passed through some invisible barrier, the scenery changes: It's now much greener and there are even some wildflowers. Huge pink dust clouds have gathered far away to the east.

At the Carnarvon Caravan Park, the Irish girl at reception is just telling me they're fully booked, when the reason arrives in the form of dozens of motorcycles. I go outside and discover that the bikes are on the Black Dog Ride from Perth to Darwin! Then David Peach, who I'd interviewed weeks before in Sydney steps out of the support vehicle and, smiling, shakes my hand. After introductions, Mal, riding a BMW 1100, kindly offers me one of the beds in his cabin and after a shower, I'm as happy as a lark, enjoying a beer and barbeque with David and his merry band. Before hitting the sack, I'm given some

Black Dog stickers for my bike.

I had a difficult relationship with my dad who was one of 26 kids (two mums; one had 16, the other had ten) born in 1929 in the East End of London. He suffered from the Black Dog and what I thought at the time was laziness, ignorance and indifference to his kids, was, I later realised – depression and anxiety. He'd hide it behind of smokescreen of macho posturing, boozing and bullying behaviour and would spend days laying on his bed feigning sickness to disguise the fact that he was fearful of facing the world. Drowning his demons in beer just like his father before him, killed him in the end. I often wonder what his life would have been like if he'd spoken to someone. My long-suffering mum loved him till the end, though we couldn't understand why. Booze and fags were his only crutch and towards the end and the only way he could view the world was through the bottom of a beer glass. I try to imagine the levels of fear and anxiety that must have gnawed away at his psyche like a rat.

I didn't attend his funeral. Living in Sydney, I lied to my mum, saying all the flights were booked. Selfishly, I couldn't face the thought of a half-empty church service full of lies and platitudes. I think of the old man as I put the Black Dog sticker on Percy's windscreen and it's his blue eyes – unreadable, and now a bit watery, that look back at me as I brush my teeth in the mirror.

It's decidedly chilly in the morning as my new friends head north and I head south for Geraldton. I'm cold all the way to the Wooramel Roadhouse, where a pasty and barely-drinkable coffee warm me up. When you do come to a small habitation or hamlet or roadhouse it's a thing to be cherished and appreciated, even if it's nothing more than a few portacabins, a dilapidated block building, some petrol bowsers and a mangy dog.

Pete, a BMW GS1200 rider joins me at my table to tell me he's riding a complete lap in just four weeks, "just to tick another box," he says before racing off. He plans to make Perth, 800 kilometres away by day's end. Inspired perhaps by my high mileage mate, I fuel up at the Overlander Roadhouse and don't stop for 270 kilometres till a sore bum forces me out of the saddle at the small settlement of

Binnu for tea and an egg sandwich. The land has changed again. The scrub has thickened into forest and turned greener. By Northampton the green is almost startling, accustomed as I've become to subtle shades of grey, red and burnt yellow. I ride through huge paddocks of wheat and granola, swaying in the sun. Sheep have replaced cattle. "We've had some good rains recently," the magnificently bearded owner of the servo tells me, "but sometimes it can be like a desert." Percy takes an age to get started and I'm at a loss as to why.

I'm amazed at how big Geraldton seems. This self-proclaimed lobster capital of the world is also famous as a top windsurfing destination. And the latter doesn't surprise me! I pull up outside the information centre to find it closed, so ride along the sea front, figuring that any backpackers would be located here and sure enough, there it is. $60 gets me a pleasant little room overlooking the main street with Wi-Fi and a TV. After visiting the supermarket, I fix myself tuna rolls with salami, olives and cherry tomatoes on the side, as I recline on my bed with a cold beer and watch Premier League football from the UK. This is the life!

After a stroll along the beach, I meet fellow resident Sam in the lounge. He's a Fijian Indian, a trained mechanic, and an entrepreneur, selling solar panels around the State. He's also partial to a drink. Over a few beers, he confidently diagnoses Percy's starting problem as dust in the carburettor and says all it needs is a good clean, a job I'm embarrassed to say I haven't the confidence to do.

I have a vivid picture of myself attempting the job and some vital spring or spacer disappearing into the gravel of the yard, never to be found again.

As I lug my gear through the lounge out to my bike next morning, I pass Sam's prostrate form, fully clothed and snoring, on a couch with an empty bottle of Jim Beam beside him. Percy starts first pop. Go figure. The countryside heading south is a green pastoral idyll. I could almost be in New Zealand's Southland. I'm heading for a tiny place called Hoddy's Well near Toodyay, about 85 kilometres inland from Perth. My mate Des Molloy, adventurer, motorcyclist and author, has put me in touch with a friend of his, Bruce, who has kindly offered to put me up and agreed to be interviewed. My GPS directs me off the Brand Highway through park-like farmland which at times resembles a giant golf course. Now in WA's

wheat belt, the riding is fantastic. I stop for lunch in the salubrious confines of the Drovers Inn in Moora, a nice little town of 1800 with tall gums in the main street providing welcome shade.

More wonderful riding brings me to the characterful town of Toodyay. This is obviously a popular spot with many motorcyclists from Perth, out for a Sunday ride. Bruce and his wife Linda soon settle me in to the spare room at Hoddy's Well and that night we eat at the Pub in Toodyay. The town, formerly known as Newcastle, was established on the River Avon in 1836, making it one of the earliest inland towns in the state. The indigenous Noongar people had called it home for millennia and it's believed the town's name was derived from the Noongar name, "Duidgee".

Meticulous Restorer
Bruce Sharman

English born Bruce, big and burly like a gentle giant, lives a life that many people would envy. Aside from residing in a beautiful little spot, his commute to work takes all of 20 seconds. And what's more, he does something he loves and is passionate about. I follow him into one of his sheds and he explains. "This is where I make electrical harnesses," he begins. "This one is for a 1953 Cadillac Eldorado," he shows me a tangled old birds nest of wires. "The customer wants me to make two new ones."

On a sheet of plywood, set up like a draughtsman's table, Bruce carefully draws the harness, accurately measuring the distances between junctions. "And of course, this one's American, so they have to do things slightly differently. It's a massive car, electric sunroof, heated seats, so the harness is complicated." Bruce shows me how he takes off all the coverings from the old harness to find the many soldered connections. Under a bench are dozens of spools of coloured wires, all different thicknesses, which must precisely match up. Then new ring terminals are made by hand from a sheet of brass and must, of course, be perfect in order to fit. They then go away and get tin-plated, before Bruce solders them on.

As he cuts new wires, he pins them to the plywood drawing and painstakingly, a new harness begins to take shape. I'm very impressed and ask him how many people are making them. "Six in the world," comes the immediate reply. "there are two in the States, two in Australia and two in England who build, what I call quality harnesses."

But the best is yet to come. Bruce then takes the harness over to a complex contraption that looks like a Steam Punk exhibit, a confusing mass of wires, levers, cogs, wheels and bobbins. Each bobbin has six strands of cotton on it, which are strung like a spider's web across tension wires. "This machine weaves a cotton braid over the wires," he says proudly, "you can't buy machines like this."

He tells me that back in the 1920's wiring harnesses on cars were all black. But as vehicles became more complex, different colours were required to identify different circuits. Lucas Industries in England started to make cables with two different colours of equal measure in them and up until World War 11, he had 33 options. With

the increased complexity of machinery, this was no longer enough, so he started to make cables with, for instance, mostly white with a small amount of red, or mostly red with a small amount of yellow, etc.

"Down there," says Bruce, "are pre-war colours of cotton with the herringbone pattern that went up to around 1960. Then they went over to PVC coated stuff. But the Americas didn't have the range of colours that Lucas had, so used the same colour for multiple circuits, making it very confusing."

"If it's confusing for you Bruce, think what it's like for me!" Bruce is famous for his wiring harnesses and experts believe he makes the best in the world. I certainly wouldn't argue. He says he prefers the English stuff and specialises in Jaguars and MG's.

We move to another shed, which has the body of a 1963 Triumph TR4 sitting on an old hospital bed which Bruce says is ideal as he can move the cars up and down. "I restore them completely, from the ground up. I take them apart and basically rebuild them. If anything needs doing, I do it. A lot of them have sentimental value you know. The car they learnt to drive in or the car their father gave them. This particular customer wants the Triumph back in concourse condition, which means show condition."

We stop by a beautiful motorcycle, an immaculate 1980 BMW R100 RS. "Man, oh man," I coo, as I caress the tank. It's an absolute work of art. "That's done just over 100,000 kilometres and has had only three owners since new," says Bruce.

Next up in the shed is a 1946 Buick with an eight-cylinder in-line motor. "The bloke brought it to me and said, 'there's no rust in it Bruce. I want it restored. And of course, there was a shit-load of rust in it." Under the hood is what looks to me like a brand-new engine. Bruce restored everything, and I marvel at his skill. I ask how long he'd expect to work on a project like this and his reply surprises me, "three to five years."

"A customer comes to me," he explains, "with a car they want restoring. Now most people can't afford $70,000 to $100,000. And that's what some cost, especially if there's a lot of rust, coz that's

where the money goes. A lot of the cars I work on, you can't buy panels, so I have to fabricate them and that takes time. And time is money."

"D'you do the painting too?" Bruce nods. "I suppose you make the tyres too?" I joke, and he shakes his head and laughs.

Bruce's rates are relatively low compared to what is charged in Perth because he lives in the country, doesn't pay rent on a premises and employs no staff. He has a system where he asks the customer what they can afford each month, works to that budget and gets on with the work. "We work our way through it. Sometimes, if they go on holiday or run low on cash, I stop and go on to another project. That's why some can take years. If I was to say to them, I want $70,000 upfront, they'd walk away. It gives me a steady income and becomes affordable for the customer and it's work that I love. Also, I never get bored because I go from project to project."

Bruce has been restoring professionally for over 10 years now and has 'go-to' people in the UK and Australia for spares. "It started out as a hobby. I restored my first Panther motorcycle when I was 24. I remember in the early '80s, going with my brother, who was picking up a Triumph Bonneville just outside London and seeing this big lump of an engine under a workbench and falling in love with it."

He bought the engine, dragged it away in a couple of Carlsberg crates and restored the Panther. "I finished it just before we emigrated to Australia and brought it across with me," he says, "and that started my love affair with Panthers."

Bruce (like my New Zealander mate Des Molloy) belongs to the Panther Owners Club. "The club," says Bruce, "is one of the best single-marque clubs in the world. If you want a part for a Panther, you can't buy it. But if you belong to the Panther Owners Club, they can probably re-manufacture it. You can buy almost anything. I can email 'Old Foxy' the spare parts guy for the club, who was visiting earlier today from England, and within a week I'll have the part."

Bruce painstakingly re-built the engine and gearbox on his 1947 600 cc Panther with mostly new parts, which he says is how he managed to ride it for nine days across to Sydney last year without any problems. Bruce and a group of friends undertook the ride under the banner of the Distinguished Gentleman's Ride and Movember, raising awareness and an amazing $20,000 for Prostate Cancer and Mental Health. "Twelve months before the ride, I took the Panther to markets and sausage sizzles and sold T-shirts. The bike was a great conversation starter. We found blokes coming up to us and saying things like, 'well I've got some problems with my water-works actually,' or, 'I've been suffering from depression.'

"On the ride rattling the tin at service stations, real conversations about these issues took place. After the ride, we wanted to make a movie but about the ride but soon realised that it wasn't about the ride, it was about the conversations, on the road and around the campfire. So, the movie we're making is about people's stories – people's personal accounts of bad things that have happened and how they've coped."

Woven into the movie, which Bruce plans to make available to groups and organisations as a resource, will be Go-Pro footage of the ride and an explanation of why they undertook it.

"We discovered that there are an awful lot of people out there, suffering from anxiety and depression," says Bruce, "so hopefully the movie will encourage people to have a conversation. Just talk to a mate over coffee or join a group. It's all about having a reason to get up in the morning!"

Apart from the 1947 bike, Bruce also owns a 1953 600, a 1938 350 and is currently re-building a 1939 350. I tell him how much I envy his mechanical ability. "Well actually I'm not a mechanic George, I'm a butcher," he says, which I find hard to believe. "We could never afford to send anything to a mechanic. When I was a kid, I'd take things apart and fix them, with my dad looking over my shoulder. Just trial and error. If I couldn't get my car to go, I'd have had to hitch-hike to work."

When Bruce got sick of being a butcher he went into logistics and warehousing, which is what he did upon arriving in Australia. "Then when I was about 50," he says, "I tired of the corporate world and started restoration for a living. But I've always tinkered in my spare time. I remember I had a little Morris Minor car I'd play with. Then I found a rare Morris Minor van and completely restored it. People saw what I was doing and started asking if I could do some work for them too. So, I worked in the corporate logistics world during the week, coming home and fixing people's cars for them at the weekend."

Moving through Bruce's workshops we come to a four-cylinder, two litre Alvis with a spare wheel on the boot lid that looks like a gun turret. "Alvis were English coachbuilders," he says, "and proba-

bly made some of the best cars on the planet. There's probably only 250 of these left in the world." Bruce shows me the wooden wheel arches. "They'd hand-build a wooden frame and then put a steel skin over it," and he shows me a beautifully crafted piece of wood that I'd swear was made of plastic. "This is a door pillar made of English ash." He reckons he's not very good with wood but somehow, I doubt that. The Alvis is Bruce's own car, he's been restoring on and off for the past 15 years, which explains why bits and pieces from it are hanging all over the workshop.

"So, what would be your favourite aspect of restoration?" I ask

"Probably the wiring and the small details," comes the reply, "although there's not much money in wiring harnesses. People don't appreciate the amount of work involved and won't pay the money."

Moving on, past all manner of workbenches and weird contraptions that only an expert would recognise, we pass a half-restored 1963 Holden EH ute. Then the chassis of a very desirable 1963 Toyota Land Cruiser. "I took this whole vehicle apart using only four spanners; 10mm, 12mm, 14mm and 17mm I think they were." He tells me the customer is very particular and I can see that he has come to the right man. The motor has been re-conditioned. Everything has been seen to, right down to the bolts which have been removed and cadmium-plated. Bruce really does amazing work.

Next is a nice little car, a 1926 Austin Seven, the sort of vehicle that Laurel and Hardy used to sit in and often demolish. "This car's been in the customer's family since the mid-1930's we think," says

Bruce, "he courted his wife in it and is now in his 80s, and wanted it restored before he passed it on." Bruce lets me sit in it. It's a snug fit and the re-upholstered seat is very comfy. "That's just about to leave. Then I can start on that one," and Bruce indicates a 1929 Morris Minor overhead camshaft chassis.

I ask him if he watches those restoration shows on the Discovery Channel. "Don't talk to me about them," he says, "they do my job a disservice because they make it all look too easy! You never see all the other guys who must be working in the background."

Bruce lets the dust settle on his projects and I find his reasoning very interesting. "I don't clean them till they're ready to go, because every time you run your finger across them, you might put a little scratch on them. I've tried covering them up, but it doesn't stop all the dust."

Then we come to Bruce's motorcycles. I admire a half-finished sidecar. "I just finished restoring a 1935 Panther. The owner took it away last week, then rang me as said, 'I think I'd like you to build me a side-car for it, Bruce.'" There are shelves and racks full of Panther engines and bits and pieces.

Panthers were originally designed to be attached to a sidecar, providing cheap post-war transport in austerity-struck Britain until the likes of Minis and Morris Minors came along. The nickname, 'sloper' comes from the distinctively sloped engine, which forms an integral part of the motorcycle's frame

"I love them. They use such simple engineering," he says as he, almost reverently unveils his lovely 1938, 350cc Panther. The tank is gorgeous and the fishtail exhaust pipes, which Bruce is at pains to point out, are not strictly correct, look like something out of Stingray. It's one of the nicest bikes I've ever seen. "Most of these parts are hand-made," he says, "because the Panther club make bugger-all for the 350s which are the lightweights. It's a simple, single-cylinder motor with a single carb and twin exhaust pipes. But it's so light. And great fun to ride."

I love workshops like this and would like to just sit down, breathe in the smell of oil and soak up the atmosphere. Bruce likes to listen to music while he beavers away, and our tastes are very similar. '70s and '80s stuff like Dylan, The Stones, Neil Young and Led Zeppelin. He's a fascinating and likeable guy and apart from his restorations, he also belongs to various clubs, paints military figures and is a keen gardener and bird watcher. I shake my head enviously, "Jesus, you've got it made mate!" I say, and he has to agree. "Yep I've got a pretty good life."

In the morning I follow Bruce on his beloved 1947 Panther, through wonderfully green wheat fields on great biking roads and I'm happy to sit on 80-90 kph. In fact, I'm copacetic! At the small town of Dowerin, we have a final chat over coffee before Bruce returns home to his many interests. According to my GPS, I've only 230 kilometres to ride today so cross the High Street and read at a picnic table in the warm sunshine. Dowerin seems like a ghost town. Like a lot of towns in the wheat belt, labour-saving machinery has killed off so many jobs, denuding towns of workers and their spending power. Many face an existential crisis. Not for the first time, I wonder what the future will bring, for without 'labour' or a purpose, what's left for the Western World apart from endless leisure. The afternoon sees me and Percy pass many huge grain silos, most I'm told, owned by CBH (Co-Operative Bulk Handling). I cruise through Wyakatchem and Trayning, a name derived from the Aboriginal "Duri-ining" meaning, "snake crawling in grass near campfire." The last section of my ride is on smooth red dirt and if my bike were a red kelpie, I feel his ears would have pricked-up in anticipation. Scores of bright green, ring-necked parrots dart across the track like a welcoming committee, just ahead of me. My good friend and neighbour Ralph, a sprightly 93, gave me his granddaughter's contact details and she and her husband promptly offer me a bed for the night on their 10,000-acre wheat farm near Talgomine.

I spend the night comfortably ensconced in a port-a-cabin or, 'donga' just up the track from the farmhouse, having enjoyed dinner and the convivial atmosphere of Melissa and Jason's young family. Birdsong wakes me up and I'm greeted with the sight of the first grey sky of the trip. Over coffee and toast, Jason and Melissa educate me on wheat farming. They grow Mace and Septer, varieties of 'hard' wheat, high in protein and ideal for top quality baking. "Meriden buys all our wheat," says Jason sipping his coffee, "which ends up in South East Asia and the Middle East. This year we've had some rain and we're expecting a good harvest of maybe 6,000 tonnes, which is a great improvement on last year."

I read the other day that, according to the UN, wheat production needs to increase by 60% in the next 30 years to help feed a predicted population of 10 billion. Some argue that there's plenty of food in the world – it's just a question of distribution.

I've wrapped and duct-taped my GPS in a Ziploc bag and struggled into my full wet weather gear for the forecast rain ahead. I've also stuffed all my gear into black bin-liners inside my soft panniers, which are not waterproof. If James Lee Burke, one of my favourite authors, was here, he'd probably describe this Australian sky as resembling 'oily rags.'

I plan on following my GPS's instructions, zig-zagging 563 kilometres south, down minor roads to Albany on the coast. I've been so lucky with the weather thus far, that the rain seems like a personal affront. I thankfully regain the tarmac before the dirt turns to mud and ride roughly south through wheat and sheep country. With good, waterproof gear, riding in the rain isn't so bad. The worst aspect is the poor visibility through your rain speckled and often steamed-up visor and of course, bends, which must be given more respect and taken a bit slower. Personally, I'm not a fan of riding in the wet, but I know some riders who love it. It takes all sorts.

Despite the rain, the ride to Kulin, where I stop for coffee is great. In a café I'm served a warm mug of milky coffee by a big, 40-some-

thing, ex-rugby type. His smokes are squashed into the top pocket of his polo shirt and his gut hangs over his belt. He is a blunt and unappealing character. "What d'ya wanna go to Albany for?" he asks as he takes my money.

"Because I haven't been there before," I feel obliged to reply, though he's not really listening to an answer.

"Huh!" he tuts, "OK if you like wind and rain I s'pose." As he serves another customer, muttering something about, 'the lousy Government and Muslims,' I move away to avoid listening to his negative rants. His slack-jawed and willful ignorance makes me shake my head and I take a perverse pleasure in leaving a nice puddle on the ground around my table. Outside, the rain may be letting up. I've found that the mere glimpse of blue in a cloudy sky can be more appealing than a whole dome of blameless blue: Rather like a tantalising glimpse of cleavage compared to a naked Playboy spread.

The rain has stopped by the time I kick my side stand down for lunch at the lovely-looking old Dumbleyung Tavern. The little town, population 225, whose name sounds like an invention of J. K. Rowling, is best known for the nearby Dumbleyung Lake where Donald Campbell broke the World Water Speed Record in 1964 in his speedboat Bluebird.

The last couple of hours riding to the coast are now dry but tremendously windy. The quaint and cosy YHA Hostel is mostly empty – just as I like it. I have an eight-bed dormitory to myself and spread my wet gear all over the place, reminding me of my daughter's bedroom. After a cold 'supermarket' supper of scotch eggs, tomatoes and olives in the empty common room I turn in.

I'm excited to be in Albany for the first time as I've heard good things about it. My namesake (and possible ancestor) Major Edmund Lockyer arrived here on the brig Amity on Christmas day in 1826 with 20 troops and 23 convicts under his command. He claimed Western Australia for the crown and soon established the first European settlement in the west of the great continent. The planting of the Union Jack here obviously brought great change to the Minang people who had lived here for millennia. Their land was known as

Kinjarling or "the place of rain" and I can certainly see why, as I head into town in the morning drizzle. The Minang people were happy to co-operate with the British military post, exchanging firewood and water for flour and sugar. But as they became more dependent on European food, their ancient culture was gradually eroded. And re-reading that, I must say, it's probably the most simplistic and naïve description of the plight of indigenous people ever written!

Purchasing a $2 beanie from the Opportunity Shop, I traipse down to the waterfront where the 44-year-old, full-sized replica of the Amity sits. As I walk, I realise that I haven't seen an Aboriginal face since Geraldton. The replica ship is amazingly cramped below decks and I'm glad I didn't have go to sea in it! I tip my hat to the bravery of those who did. The brig, two-masted with square sails, was the maritime workhorse of the day and the Amity was the smallest of the 'square riggers' at 142 tons.

In the afternoon I drop Percy off for another service and ask the Kawasaki mechanic to give the carburettor a good cleanout. He seems very competent and I'm heartened by the fact that two new KLR's sit in the front of the shop. He's as mystified as I am by the intermittent starting problem and offers to clean the brushes on the starter motor too.

I'm currently reading the marvellous history of humankind, Sapiens by Yuval Noah Harari. I draw a few stares when I burst out laughing like a crazy person at my table in a nice coffee shop opposite the Townhall. Harari tells the story of the Apollo 11 astronauts Armstrong and Aldrin, training in the remote, barren desert in the western United States prior to the 1969 moon landing. An ancient, gnarly Native American man approached them and asked them what they were up to. When they told him, he asked them to do him a favour. He said his tribe believed that holy spirits lived on the Moon and if they met any, would they please pass on a message from his people. The two astronauts said they'd be honoured to. The old man said something in his tribal language and got the two astronauts to repeat it back to him till they had it off pat. "I cannot tell you what it means as it is a secret, only the Moon spirits are allowed to hear," he said. Back at Mission Control the astronauts eventually found somebody who could translate the tribal language but were a bit perplexed when the translator fell about laughing. Apparently, the message they had memorized so well meant, "Don't believe a single word these people are telling you. They have come to steal your lands."

I thoroughly enjoy my couple of days exploring, reading and relaxing and as I clunk Percy into gear (he started first pop) and let out the clutch, I promise myself I'll return, hopefully when the sun is shining. I have my full wet-weather gear on but although it's cool and windy, the rain doesn't eventuate. Once more, the wind is dangerously gusty. After an extremely long stretch of straight road, I fuel up in Ravensthorpe. In a café I make myself at home – I take my riding gear off, put my tank bag on the table and open my book. The lady, a chubby 40-something, brings my coffee in a take-away cup.

"Can I have a proper cup please?" I ask.

"People usually have take-away cups," she replies matter-of-factly.

"But I'm sitting here in the café and you've got proper cups on top of the machine," I point out. Now she looks pissed-off which I think is ridiculous. Then she brings my toasted sandwich out in a brown paper bag, when plates are stacked on the counter. I sit there for another 20 minutes unable to concentrate on my book as a speaker is blaring shit pop music and mindless adverts above my head.

Back in the saddle of my KLR, my mood improves, as I knew it would. If I could only communicate a fraction of the sense of high spirits a solo journey by motorcycle conveys. You instantly replace society's straight-jacket of conformity with your biking gear, hit the road, get your wheels turning (metaphorically and literally) and charge-up your own Chakra! (for those uninitiated among you, that's your purple one). The thing that adds spice to it is the fact that anything can happen. Instead of watching a movie on your widescreen plasma, it's you out there, eating bugs and diesel fumes, getting hot or wet or cold, meeting new people, and generally challenging and putting yourself at risk. You can escape the often, soul-deadening routine of what we term, 'normal life.' Gradually, as you twist that throttle and lean into a bend, your spirit lightens, and you can laugh at the comedy that is life!

As I laugh inside, the final 200 kilometres of the day flash by. The Esperance YHA hostel is located right by an amazingly long beach of squeaky, white sand. I get my own little room, like a Bed and Breakfast room from the '70s, for $45. I polish off the stale bread, tin of tuna and squashed bananas from the meagre pantry that sits in my right saddlebag, as my fellow hostellers, a middle-aged Korean couple in a hire car, look on pityingly. They animatedly tuck into a delicious looking spread of noodles, vegetables and chicken. At the pub that night I sink a couple of pints of Kosiosku lager while some locals try to teach me the finer points of AFL, which is playing above the bar. They tell me Esperance is very popular in the summer and people visit from far and wide. It's the 'local' beach for residents of Kalgoorlie, 390 kilometres to the north. Australia is big!

It's raining in the morning, so I decide to stay put for another day. The rather large Samoan warden is surprised that I'm happy to walk the 30 minutes into town rather than ride. I buy a cheap sleeping bag in a camping shop to go inside my thin summer one as a frost is forecast for tomorrow in Norseman, a town I plan to pass through.

In the early 1820s, Australia's only pirate, Black Jack Anderson called this area home, carrying on in piratical fashion, raiding ships and looking after his harem of Aboriginal women, whose husbands he had murdered.

I stop in the nice little museum and learn that pieces of the first Space Station, Skylab crashed onto the town in 1979 when it burned up in the atmosphere. Apparently, the Municipality fined the US Government $400 for littering and eventually received payment (with no interest for late payment) in 2009. The San Francisco Examiner offered a $10,000 prize for the first person to bring a piece of the space debris into its office. Enterprising Esperance resident, 17-year-old Stan Thornton immediately grabbed a piece from his roof, caught the first flight out and claimed the prize. I wonder what he's up to today?

Chapter Eight.

THE NULLARBOR

*"In the desert in the dry.
Sun sits so high."*
Midnight Oil

H eading north east towards the famed Nullarbor, the landscape morphs slowly from scrub and forest into vast areas of wheat, punctuated by mulga and mallee. Back in the 1930's unenlightened European farming practices added to years of drought, transformed this area into a dust bowl, with salt rising to the surface and precious topsoil disappearing with the wind. Over the decades Government scientists planted gum trees, salt-friendly mulga and other native scrub in an effort to secure the soil. They were successful, and the result is the productive wheat growing land I now ride through.

At Salmon Gums Roadhouse, the young lady serving me smiles beautifully and I mirror it automatically like a chameleon or a Siamese fighting fish. Smiles like that can make your day I think to myself as I sip my coffee. What a gift, to be able to lift a stranger's spirits with such minimal effort. I feel sure that if I were to try and smile beautifully at the next person I meet, they'd either send for a cop or a nurse. The owner, a competent looking 40-something woman in worn overalls, who I've been watching on a scaffold on

the forecourt re-wiring some lights, comes in for a chat. She asks how my coffee is and I lie and tell her it's good. She spent 20 years as an electrical engineer in the Royal Australian Navy, she tells me and had returned to Salmon Gums where she was born and bred, to try and make a go of the servo. As I leave I wish her luck.

    I pull into Norseman, at around noon as the sun bursts through the clouds. I see some tin camel sculptures on the roundabout and park my bike beside them for a photo as a kind faced and chatty lady wanders by and offers to takes the picture with me in it. She works in the tourism industry and is well versed in local history. "Camels," she informs me in tone that seems well rehearsed, "and these are dromedarys, with one hump, were brought here in the late 1800's, along with their Afghan handlers and were used extensively in the region for all the donkey work." There are now hundreds of thousands of wild camels roaming WA, which are regularly herded up and shipped to the Arab world.

    After bacon and eggs, I fill up with fuel, unload the bike and tighten and lubricate the chain, before heading off on the Eyre Highway to cross the Nullarbor, a plain that rose out of the ocean 25 million years ago. Beneath the metre of soil lies between 15 and 60 metres of limestone from dead sea creatures. The Nullarbor had always been on my "roads to ride" bucket list. I had crossed it before in the opposite direction in rather unspectacular fashion on a

Greyhound bus 38 years ago and think I fell asleep, waking up with a sore neck. But what was a bore, sitting on a bus is transformed into an amazing experience on two wheels.

The road has a real "outback" feel to it again, which I haven't experienced since leaving Geraldton to the north. There is road kill once more, grey 'roos mostly, with the attendant kites doing their best to clean up the mess. The road of course is dead straight. Way above me another wedge tailed eagle has found a thermal to soar on in a seemingly limitless sky. I take a photo of a sign declaring the longest section of straight road in Australia at 90 miles or 146.6 kms. It's slide rule straight! And just as well as I have plenty of time to slow to a stop to let a huge emu shepherd his six chicks across the highway. I say "his" because unlike most species, it's the male emu who looks after the young, while the female wanders off in search of another mate.

The Road. Ever the road. The only other place I can compare to this unique emptiness is Baluchistan in Pakistan, whose sandy wastes my mate Chog and I crossed in 1983, heading for India. But I remember people popping up from nowhere riding bicycles or strolling along as though shopping on the High Street. The only chance of seeing human beings not behind a wheel out here is if

they're taking a pee beside their campervan or taking a photo of the landscape. Sometimes on these long stretches it's hard to believe that there exists a world outside of this empty landscape and dotted white lines. But thinking of that make you realise, the bubble that your senses experience in the present is in fact the entire universe. Before I can get too metaphysical in my thoughts, I'm brought down to earth by the need to pee. I pull over and watch the thirsty soil drink up my urine.

There are far less Grey Nomads, cashed up Baby Boomers and retirees, down here in the south. Perhaps because the winter has something of a bite to it compared the perpetual summer of the north. As I write notes a familiar green 250 Ninja pulls up, ridden by smiling Titsuo, a 41-year-old Japanese guy, I've been playing leap-frog with since Albany. He's no stranger to the Nullarbor, having cycled across it a few years back. He also rode a 49cc moped, across it. He has two huge bags strapped precariously to the back of his bike and looking to me as though they're always about to fall off. (I give him a wide berth when overtaking)

The monochromatic nature of the landscape, with a unique beauty all its own washes over me like a benediction. The tarmac stretches on, ever on, as though I'm inside a video game. I long for

a curve in the road, or a cloud in the perfect pale blue dome of the sky. At the Balladonia Roadhouse 187 k's east, where another piece of Skylab sits proudly on the roof, I book into a very basic room for $50. It's like a tiny port-a-cabin, complete with red dust on every surface but the sheets are clean. I could have camped for $25 but would have needed a sledge hammer for my tent pegs.

In the bar I watch the All Blacks romp home against the Wallabies (no surprises there) with contractors who are working on the road. Baz from Napier in New Zealand tells me they're maintaining the shoulders of the Highway, four k's per day, both sides. He drives the roller to compact the sand and gravel and uses 40,000 litres of water, draughted from local bores to dampen it down. He also insists on buying me cans of Emu beer which isn't a bad drop at all. They're good company but I can't compete with their beer drinking.

Declining the offer of more beer, I remember reading somewhere that temptation resisted is a true measure of character. So, feeling a bit self-righteous I thrash myself on the back with a birch twig a few times before crawling, monk-like under my blankets in my tiny room. Wordsmith Kingsley Amiss, who was once quoted as saying his hangover was so bad that his hair hurt, had a sure-fire cure for a hangover, which was downing a glass of Bovril and vodka! Another suggestion of his was to take a 30-minute ride in an open topped aircraft (preferably flown by a sober pilot).

I rely on a pint of water, eggs on toast, coffee and a bracing ride in the cold morning air. About 80 k's down the road, I give Baz and his fellow road workers a toot and a cheery wave and accelerate away in a swirl of red dust. To give you an idea of the scale of the Nullarbor (and indeed Australia), Edward John Eyre (of the Eyre Highway fame) took five arduous months to become the first European to cross the arid plain from East to West in 1840/41. When Eyre and his native tracker Wyle finally arrived in Albany, having been given up for dead, Eyre wept and reflected on his three other comrades who had perished on the awful journey.

I see ahead what looks like a grey boulder, but on closer inspection turns out to be a dead camel. There are also the tell-tale black

rubber tracks leading up to it, evidence of a road train slamming on its anchors. The Nullarbor is far less bleak and featureless than I'd realised. The bush is ever changing. Roughly 50 species of eucalypts thrive in the arid conditions of the Nullarbor, from small coppery, slender gimlets to scrubby mallee and the sometimes 25-metre-tall salmon gums. There's also a huge variety of other shrubs and trees, not just gums and acacias. Flowering plants include saltbush, bluebush and wattle are common too. These bloom mainly between September and February but as John Williamson sings in Ancient Mountains, "Where spring will come with any rain; a chance to flower and seed again." And now of course, that ear-worm will be with me for days.

It is suggested that Aboriginal people lived along the Nullarbor as far back as 18,000 years ago but populations were sparse, as little as one person per 100 square kilometers. The first contact with the indigenous inhabitants of the region occurred around 1866 when pastoralists arrived to 'develope' the land. The inevitable influx of more European settlers and missionaries gradually threatened the traditional lifestyle and practices of the Aboriginals and as tribal elders died, knowledge of law, language and culture died with them. An all too familiar tale.

At the Eucla Roadhouse, with 522 effortless kilometres under my belt, I book into a cabin at the attached Eucla Motor Motel. The room is a lot cleaner than last night's one. Leaning against the wall of the room next door is an impressive looking tandem pushbike. After a shower I catch up on some notes and download some photos, before wandering over to the bar (I told you the roadhouses were good) Here, I meet two young British Doctors, Lloyd from Wales and Louis, a Yorkshireman from Leeds who are playing pool. When I ask them if they're riding the tandem, they nod and join me at the table where I'm working my way through a burger and a huge mound of chips. My Dictaphone appears as if by magic.

World Tandem Riders
Lloyd and Louis

Louis Snellgrove and Lloyd Collier are a great pair of lads; the kind that girls would love to bring home and introduce to their parents. They are both Emergency Registrars working in Townsville and are pedalling their tandem bike, not just across the Nullarbor, but around the world.

Originally Lloyd planned to ride around the world on his own but was 'over the moon' when his mate Louis decided to accompany him and suggested they ride a tandem. The charity ride for Spinal Research and the Brain Foundation, is in memory of Lloyd's uncle who recently passed away. "He broke his back when he was 29 and was confined to a wheel chair for the next 30 years," says Lloyd. "He was a hero of mine and was a wonderful human being. He never let his handicap get him down and lived life to the full, running his own haulage business, water skiing, scuba diving and quad biking."

They also decided to have a crack at the Guinness Book of Record's, 'fastest circumnavigation of the Globe by tandem bicycle,' the current record of which stands at 290 days and was achieved recently by two other British lads.

"The first part of our ride is mapped. We started 12 days ago from Adelaide and plan to make our way across to Perth, fly to Beijing, cycle to Ulaanbaatar in Mongolia and through Siberia to Novosibirsk. We then fly to Chennai in India and cycle across to Mumbai."

I tell them I was travelling around India in 1983 when Chennai was Madras, and Mumbai was Bombay and they laugh and swig beer in unison.

"The plan then is to fly to Turkey and carry on pedalling across Europe to Madrid, then down and across to Marrakesh in Morocco. We chose Madrid and Wellington as our antipodal points; a requirement for the world record. Then we fly to Florida, cycle across the States, fly to New Zealand and cycle the length and finally, fly to Brisbane and cycle back to Adelaide."

"So, we're going 29,000 kilometres," chips in Louis, "in an easterly direction. And to qualify for the record we can't use any private transportation apart from the bike."

The handsome looking bike is what the lads term a 'middle of the range' type called a Dawes Galaxy Twin and was much cheaper than I thought it would be, even given the generous discount given by the company. The lads have also spent around $2,000 on refinements and alterations, such as more robust wheels, more comfortable seats and a dynamo powered USB port. "We worked it out," Louis says, "that for every kilometre we pedal, the dynamo charges our phones 1%."

I ask them how the first 12 days have gone. "Well so far," says Lloyd, "the people of South Australia have been fabulous. This single, old farmer put us up near Port Wakefield when we were absolutely knackered. It was a great night around a roaring fire with tea and biscuits, with him telling us all about the Snow Town murders, which had happened nearby."

Lloyd and Louis have been blown away by the hospitality they've been shown. Two nights ago, at the Nullarbor Roadhouse, a lady asked if she could take a selfie with the two lads, who happily obliged. When they went inside to book a room for the night, they were told that the same lady had already paid for it and driven off. "It's little things like that that really make our day," Louis says.

The tandem riders prefer to camp wherever possible and have enjoyed some great nights so far, on secluded beaches. The wind has been their greatest challenge and I sympathise with them. I've only got to stay upright, but they must pedal against it! "Yesterday we covered 160 kilometres," Lloyd says, "but that was going into the wind. We're 200 kilos between us plus our gear so it's a quite a lump to pedal! And I've been struggling with a knee injury, so to be fair, Louis has probably been doing more work these last five days."

"Did you do any training before you started?" I ask.

"We entered an Iron Man competition in Cairns before the trip, so we did a bit," Louis replies.

"When we were training for the Iron Man," Lloyd says, "I ran five k's in six minutes, forty-five seconds and the other day near Port Augusta, it was so windy we managed five k's in twenty-five minutes!"

During windy periods like that, the lads must stop every ten kilometres and eat something as it's so energy sapping but they're confident that their bodies are acclimatising.

They carry eight litres of water in bladders which are built into the frame of the bike plus a water bottle each. A basic tool kit is carried plus puncture repair kits, spare inner tubes and tyres, spare chain and brake cables.

They are both at pains to stress that the money raised by their ride will go to the unsung heroes, working behind the scenes who do the research. Because without them there can be no advancement in medicine. "The Brain Foundation is Australian and Spinal Research is British," says Lloyd, "so we thought it would be a nice link between the two."

Once again it has been a pleasure to meet such committed and inspirational people, who I wish Bon Voyage and let them get back to their pool game.

The first crossing of this vast emptiness by motorized vehicle was achieved in 1912 by S.R. Ferguson of NSW, his companion and mechanic Francis Birtles and fox terrier Rex, driving an American contraption called a Brush. The single cylinder, 10 horsepower car had a slender hickory frame and achieved a top speed of 20 mph. The intrepid trio set off from Freemantle, heading for Sydney with a fortnight's supply of tinned food, four water-bags and a pocket compass. Tyres, oil and petrol had been deposited along the route for them. They carried no spare parts or even a spare wheel. At Coolgardie they left the railway line they'd been driving on and headed East on a well-worn camel track across a grim and wild four hundred miles of scrub and desert to Eucla. They then limped across the 1000 miles of limestone plateau, which a generation later became one of the best natural-surfaced roads in Australia, following the wheel ruts left by the buggies of the telegraph line maintenance crews, often digging out and dragging the bogged vehicle by rope between each pole. Dingoes trailed after them and kept them awake at night with their howling.

When the big end fractured, they cut up the push bike Birtles had strapped to the Brush to repair it and when a wooden axle broke near Broken Hill the adventurers cut up two screwdrivers to make pins for it. They arrived in Sydney to a hero's welcome, 28 days and 2,600 miles later. By 1924 only three more cars had made the journey.

Before heading off, and grateful I can merely twist my right hand and don't have to pedal, I wander over to the ruins of the Eucla Telegraph Station in the morning sun. It's very chilly and I'm putting off getting on the bike if I'm honest. The ruins are just behind the Roadhouse. The first east-west telegraph line took two and a half years to complete and in 1877 the two wires were joined on this spot. The first message, "Eucla line opened. Hurrah!" followed shortly after.

The South Australian border and Border Village are only twelve kilometres up the road. I take the obligatory photo of the huge kangaroo holding a jar of vegemite, presiding over a Christmas tree of signs, one of which tells me that Paris is 17,204 kilometres away. I swing my leg over Percy once more and press on; now into the Nul-

larbor National Park. The Aboriginal name for the Park is "Oondiri" meaning "waterless." I enjoy some great riding in the morning, the tactile and audible thump, thump, thump of my KLR mixing with the crashing waves of the Great Australian Bight on my right.

There are a few dirt roads leading to parking areas and board walks to observation spots where you can look down the coast and see the huge Bunda Cliffs, up to 90 metres above the waves, marching off into the distance. It gives me a thrill, knowing that to my left, there is nothing but parched wilderness for thousands of kilometres, up past Uluru and all the way to Darwin.

The accepted size of the Nullarbor is the huge 1,200 kilometre stretch from Norseman to Ceduna, which has taken me two and a half days of magic riding. That's what it says on the sticker I bought at the Roadhouse anyway.

In 1865 Edmund Delisser, a surveyor, aptly named the flat plain, the Nullarbor, from nullus arbor (which is Latin for "no trees"). I discover, thanks to a free map I picked up back in Balladonia, that the actual "Nullarbor" or "Tree-less plain" is entirely in South Australia.

I fuel and coffee up in the Nullarbor Roadhouse, where I bump into Titsuo again on his 250 Ninja. He's taken my advice and now rides at 100 kph, giving him much better fuel economy. He explains this to me with an impressive display of sign language. I reckon he'd

be a great man to have on your team if you're playing charades. Scenic flights are available here to view the southern right whales, so named because in the 1800's they were the "right" whales to hunt. I'm pleased to read that numbers are steadily on the rise due to their status as a protected species.

More great riding follows, with glimpses of civilization, like enormous wheat fields. I stop at the Nundroo Roadhouse, which is like a museum piece from the 70's, complete with nasty coffee in a take-away-cup. I'm served by a shy young Indian lady who seems so pathetically grateful for my custom, that I also buy a piece of dried up fruit cake from the unappealing display on the shelves.

The morning slopes into afternoon and before I know it I've ridden the last 150 kilometres on autopilot through bush and wheat and sheep country. As the sun sets behind me, I chase my shadow back to the sea and a Caravan Park in the picturesque sea-side town of Ceduna. At the Supermarket I ask the young girl behind the Deli counter for 100 grams of stuffed olives. She fills a plastic container and says, "there's 220 in here; is that OK?"

"No," I say, "I only want 100 thanks."

"Oh," she says, stumped, "d'ya want me to take some out then?"

Back at the Caravan Park, with a cold beer in hand, I kick off my boots, put my socks outside to get some air, put my feet up and reflect on the last few days. People (mostly armchair travellers) had warned me of the perils of the Nullarbor; kamikaze wildlife, merciless weather and hurricane winds among the perils. But really, though the bush was spectacular, it was just a long ride. Ted Simon, doyen of motorcycle travellers best summed up the warnings in his classic book, Jupiters Travels. "Australians in cities," he wrote, "love to shudder at the merciless hostility of their continent. I wondered whether it was a sort of apology for betraying the national ideal, an excuse for not being out there digging."

The Eyre Peninsula, which I enter this morning is a 170,500 square kilometer triangle of land known as Australia's 'Seafood Frontier.' It's bigger than Nepal and slightly smaller than Uruguay, which again gives an idea of the scale of this huge country, which every school kid knows, is the 6th largest on Earth. I spot an idyllic sandy beach at Streaky Bay and ride down for a closer look, only to get my bike stuck in the soft sand. I unload everything in the growing heat and pack seaweed under the tyres. As I stamp it down, I hear a crunch and realise that I've just crushed my sunnies! I manage to get out, now wearing my spare ones (which are rubbish), only to drop Percy when I turn toward firmer ground. Eventually, after much huffing, puffing, sweating and straining of my repaired hernias, I leave the beach and give a sarcastic wave to the old geezer who has been silently watching the free entertainment from a nearby sand dune.

I ride on through vast wheat fields and rocky, sheep filled paddocks to Elliston, another attractive little sea-side town, popular with surfers. As I sit in the sun sipping a good flat white, a couple walking their kelpie stop and we chat about dogs. The country reminds me of the Yorkshire Moors, complete with dry stone walls. Approaching Port Lincoln, one of the world's largest natural harbours and sea-food capital of Australia, I pass huge paddocks of canola swaying in the wind. I've arranged to stay with and interview another acquaintance of my brother-in-law Ken.

Again, I'm taken aback by the generosity of people who don't know me from a bar of soap. Hagen and his delightful wife Anna put me up in a spare room in the palatial home they built together, whose glass front, huge deck and pool overlook Boston Bay.

Tuna Baron
Hagen Stehr

I'm sitting with Hagen in his kitchen with a cold beer. He drinks very strong, black, instant coffee. "I've tried all that fancy coffee but just prefer it," he says, "and I usually get through around fifteen cups a day." I can see how he could easily be intimidating to some. He's built like a brick shit-house and despite his 75 years, gives the impression of barely restrained power. Although polite and articulate, you get the impression that he's not a man to trifle with.

He was born in what was then Prussia and comes from a long line of Military men. "My parents were in the Hitler Youth. They were Nazis through and through. After the loss in the war, my father escaped to Egypt as the Americans were after him and joined the military over there. But after a couple of years in the Egyptian military he returned to West Germany as a chemist."

"Well your story certainly started off with a bang Hagen!" I tell him.

Hagen hated the military-like discipline in the house and often felt as though he were merely excess baggage. In 1955 his parents, now divorced decided the best way to instil some discipline into young Hagen, who admits he was difficult to handle, was to pack him off to Naval School. "I was 12 years old," Hagen says, "and I was enrolled in an Officer Cadetship in the Navy. Later I sailed to South America on the Pamir as one of the Merchant Marine trainees, which is where I jumped ship and returned to Europe."

The Pamir was a four masted Barque, seized as a prize of war by the New Zealand Government in 1941. It was famous for being the last commercial sailing ship to round Cape Horn in 1949. It sank in 1957 of the Azores, overwhelmed by Hurricane Carrie.

"Of course," continues Hagen, "I couldn't return home as my family didn't like me very much. I'd dishonoured the Stehr name."

After knocking around for a while in Holland and France sixteen-year-old Hagen walked into the Gare du Nord in Paris and saw the tiny recruitment office for the French Foreign Legion. "The only thing they wanted to know was what I wanted to be known as. There were lots of Germans joining up. They told me to sign a form and bang, just like that I'd joined for a five-year stint. Back then in 1959 they'd take anybody. If you were on the run," he says, "they'd sign you up. It's a lot more difficult now. I think that for every thousand applicants today, only fifty get in."

I was young and fit but basic training was fucking hard. I think it lasted around five months, in Algeria, Morocco's Atlas Mountains and Crete. But Germans controlled the Foreign Legion. Back then, we sang German songs and the commands were given in German and English. But the worst people I found were the French from Alsace-Lorraine. They were Germans one day and French the next!"

Legionnaires were paid in cash, which Hagen says had to be stashed under the mattress as bank accounts were unheard of. A lot of guys left to fight in Cuba for Fidel Castro as they were being paid the huge sum of US$300 per month. Hagen went to Cuba himself, but the fighting was over by the time he arrived. An old school mate of his fought for Castro against Batista and stayed on to become a

Colonel in the Cuban Army.

"But let me tell you George, there was no mystique in being a Legionnaire. It was brutal. It was a hard slog. It was hard work."

Hagen's parents found it disgraceful that their son was now fighting for the French and was persona non grata in their eyes. It would be ten years before he spoke to them again. After almost a year of Legion discipline Hagen had had enough and went AWOL, ending up, after adventures too numerous to mention, in Casablanca. "If they had caught me, I would have been shot."

He then joined a merchant ship and sailed to South America to retrieve his papers. He says, "I could work on ships, no problem, but without papers, I couldn't stay in a country for more than 30 days."

Hagen's wife Anna then brings in a book; Australians in the French Foreign Legion and there, inside we find Hagen's photograph. "I feel very honoured to appear in there," he says. "I then signed on a Panamanian ship and worked around the far east in Japan, South Korea and Vietnam."

He set eyes on Australia for the first time, hauling phosphate from Nauru to Geelong and on to Port Lincoln. "Jesus it was a hick town in those days," he says, "swinging doors and fist fights. I felt right at home!"

His ship was in Port Lincoln for six weeks, in which time Hagen made many useful contacts, some of whom suggested that he stay. "So, on our last day, I packed my bag, walked to the top of the hill and watched my ship sail for Liverpool."

The following day, 18-year-old Hagen reported to the Police Station (along with half a dozen other sailors) and was told that he wasn't supposed to be there. "I think I had about thirty shillings on me," he says as he finishes off his coffee. "I don't really know how I got in to be honest George. I washed the police cars and did some gardening. They put me up in the pub and I had to go to Court a few times. That's where I met Anna, who was working there. Back then, the plane flew in from Adelaide once a week, so we had to wait a whole month before the Immigration guys came to talk to us."

"Eventually the Mayor said to Hagen and the other sailors, 'if you don't get drunk, you can stay here for six months," adds Anna (Australian born from Greek heritage) and they were given stamped papers to that effect.

"And of course, I became an Aussie when Anna and I were married," Hagen says. "The first thing she ever said to me was, 'please make love to me?!'" Hagen says and winks.

"Not true!" says Anna and they fall about laughing at the memories.

"But seriously," he says, "it was the best move of my life. Not only did I meet my lovely wife, but I came to live in the Lucky Country, the best country in the world!"

It was the start of the tuna season, so Hagen decided to ask for a job on one of the fishing boats, a decision that would take him to the very top of the industry. Back then, long poles baited with squid were used, a method that could land as much as 70 tons of tuna in five hours.

"I soon worked my way up the line and had a bit of luck. I thought I'd probably stay a couple of years. That was 57 years ago. I'm constantly travelling all over the world," he says, "and the only place as good as this in my opinion is Queenstown in New Zealand."

Hagen took to fishing like a duck to water and soon built his first boat, followed by a two-year stint diving for abalone. He says as far as he knows, he was the only abalone fisherman in the country who worked alone. He'd strap on his mask, start the pump and jump overboard. If the pump stopped, he'd have to come up. "But I dived on dangerous reefs where nobody else would go. In those days, you'd get about 40 cents a kilogram. My licence cost about two dollars but a licence sold recently for 13 million! Just for a piece of paper."

Hard work came naturally to Hagen (who also took up heavyweight boxing for a spell) and he thrived. As well as tuna fishing, he had a crack at lobster fishing and trawling for prawns but didn't like it.

It was tuna fishing that Hagen really saw a future in. After hauling tuna for other operators for a decade, he formed his own company and started to build his own fleet and reputation.

"The tuna industry really started in the early 60's with the arrival of Croatian immigrants," Hagen explains. "It soon crystallised itself into a very powerful industry, with companies trying to carve out their own niche. It's now controlled by four major families, of which mine is one. We've been called all sorts of things, like the 'Port Lincoln Mafia' but that's only natural I suppose."

Hagen pauses while he gets me another beer. "There was a lot of money made here. I think there are more millionaires living a mile from this house than anywhere in the country. And it used to be just a tiny hick town!"

Hagen stresses that all the wealth only came to pass because of the quota system introduced from New Zealand, which protected the fish stocks and allowed the price to go up.

While others preferred to keep a low profile, Hagen, never one to be shy of coming forward, campaigned for better conditions and lobbied the Government to provide proper training for crews. His voice was eventually heard (and I can imagine he can be quite persuasive) and 23 years ago the Australian Maritime and Fisheries Academy was set up in Adelaide. Hagen was asked to become its Chairman, a position he still holds today. It's the largest Academy of its kind in the country, is industry run and is largely funded by Hagen himself. Many courses are available at the Academy, from Coxswain Courses and Shipboard Safety, to Engineering to Marine Rescue.

"Australia has been very good to me," he says, "so I thought I'd give something back. It's something that's very, very important to me and I'm very proud of it."

"So, does it take up much of your time Hagen?"

"Quite a bit, yes. My own business has grown and today my son Marcus is taking over more and more, but I keep a close eye on it. I think we've got 18 or 19 tuna boats now, based here in Port Lincoln."

Often referred to as the "Tuna King" or "The Kaiser", his achievements and accolades are far too numerous to mention. He belongs to several other boards and committees, including being the Ambassador of Indigenous Employment Projects. As well as being a qualified pilot and previously owning a parachute jumping school, Hagen is a prolific writer. His monthly column, "Stehring the Kaiser" for Ausmarine magazine is always eagerly anticipated in the industry.

Hagen was awarded Officer of the Order of Australia on Australia day 1997 for service to the commercial fishing industry and to education and training. "The highest honour ever awarded to a fisherman," says Anna proudly.

"If we had lived in New Zealand," says Hagen, I would have been a 'Sir.'"

His company Clean Seas Tuna became the first to create an artificial breeding regime for Southern Blue fin Tuna, a milestone Time magazine rated as the 2nd best invention of 2009. "Our company was the first one in the world to close the life cycle of tuna and kingfish George."

Hagen the visionary found a way to breed his own tuna, dispensing with the need to take them from the wild stocks, starting the world's first bluefin tuna hatchery in nearby Arno Bay. Before this, the tuna were wrangled from the ocean and held in huge cages containing up to 4000 fish. Inside these cages, anchored in Boston Bay, the fish grew, to be sold eventually on the Japanese fish market.

"And now we also do that with yellowtail kingfish," he adds. "It's more like fish ranching than fish farming. For doing that, the University of Sunshine Coast awarded me an honorary doctorate."

"So, should I call you 'Sir' or 'Doctor'?" I ask.

"Hagen will do!" he says with a grin and hands me another beer. "But I spent millions of dollars developing the model. That doctorate was the most expensive in the world, let me tell you!"

In 2014 Hagen acted as an ambassador for the seafood industry as part of Prime Minister Tony Abbot's trade delegation to China. I'm amazed there isn't a published biography detailing his amazing life.

Hagen Stehr remains unaffected by wealth and power and seems a great guy to have a yarn and few beers with. Often politically incorrect, he is a complex, incredibly intelligent and driven human being. He believes in God and is also a huge fan of World War 11 General George Patton, whose books adorn his shelves. Hagen Stehr is a force of nature.

The night before I leave, Hagen and Anna take me to a Chinese restaurant in town, along with their bubbly daughter Yasmin and her partner Mike. Yasmin, who used to fly tuna spotter planes out at sea is an interesting lady, with a burgeoning enterprise near Adelaide that allows tourists to swim with Tuna. I promise to visit it if time allows. Over dinner, Hagen entertains us with stories, of which he has a plethora. In Paris on business a few years ago he was invited to a reception at the Australian Embassy. The Ambassador introduced Hagen to a dark haired, slight man. "Nice to meet you," said Hagen, "what do you do?"

"I'm a movie star," came the reply.

"No, really. What do you do?"

"I'm a movie star," the man insisted.

After a bit more of this, Hagen, who it must be said is probably not the most patient guy on the planet, got a little bid mad and raised his voice, "what do you really do?" The day is saved by the Ambassador, who walked over and said, "Hagen, meet George Clooney."

"Who?" said Hagen. Later it was explained to him that they were filming Oceans Eleven and the crew were staying at the Embassy.

We all laugh, though I'm sure the others have heard the story before. "He wasn't very big," Hagen says. "At breakfast I discovered

that he was a Socialist and we argued for about three hours. I told the Ambassador not to sit me beside that Leftie ever again!"

In the morning Hagen asks me what I want for breakfast. "Cereal will be fine," I reply.

"Cereal, pah!" he says, "you're having bacon and eggs," and proceeds to fry up a mountain of bacon, mixed in with six eggs. "Here," he says, "putting the huge frisbee sized concoction in front of me. You need to keep your strength up."

"How come I've got six eggs and you've only got one?" I ask

"I'm watching my cholesterol!" he grins and I tuck in. Hagen is a man, not to be denied.

I've been made to feel like family in Hagen and Anna's home and leave reluctantly, dressed in my wet weather gear. Percy starts first go and we head north for Port Augusta on straight roads through wheat fields, low hills and light rain. The west side of the Eyre Peninsula, I'm told is wilder than the more populated east side. I have a cup of tea in the rather depressed looking coastal town of Arno Bay, in a café-cum-general store, where I'm the only customer sitting at a 1960's Formica table, dripping rain onto the linoleum. On the beach is a large information sign, describing Hagen's exploits.

100 kilometres of wild bush follows. I catch a movement to my left and, grabbing a hand full of front brake, manage to slow down to around 50 kph, just in time as a large emu darts out of the bushes. She runs along the road beside me for a while, before heading back into the scrub and I've just enough time to stop and photograph her. Ten minutes later a 'roo jumps across the highway not

ten metres ahead of me. Adrenalin pumping, I take it easy for the rest of the way into the town of Whyalla where I stop for a sandwich. I'm in the centre of town on a weekday afternoon but there's not a soul around and traffic is very light, which surprises me as it's the third most populous city in the state. It can get hot here in the summer and boasts a record of 49.4 degrees.

North of Wyallah the country opens up and it's as though I'm riding through the Kimberley again, with the Eire Highway cutting through dry, bush covered hills. In Port Augusta I pitch my tent in a half empty Discovery camp site for $25 and walk the three kilometres into town and the Public Library, where I take advantage of their Wi-Fi and catch up on some emails. After another cheap, cold supermarket biker's platter, I sleep, snug as a bug inside my two sleeping bags.

I'd love to wake up and spring out of bed (or in this case spring up from the ground) like a younger version of myself but have to be content to crawl out of my cocoon into a chilly morning. Sometimes the appetite for a new day is not as strong as others but I know that once I'm in motion, eating up the white lines, my mood will improve.

Bike packed, I eat a couple of bananas and some semi-stale bread as I take a last look at the small oblong of flattened grass where my tent lay and imagine it springing back up as I ride south. In town the traffic lights turn green and I twist the throttle. Instead of roaring off, Percy's motor just idles. Confused, I push the bike onto the pavement, take off my helmet and scratch my head. So invested am I in the notion of accelerating towards Adelaide, that I just stand there like a stunned mullet for about 30 seconds. This isn't in the script at all!

Wishing I was more mechanically inclined, I ride at walking pace to the nearby Information Centre as Percy will run but only at idling revs. The lady tells me that I'm in luck and not 200 metres up the road salvation awaits at Northern Motorcycles. Phil the owner seems very interested in my trip and diagnoses my problem instantly. Apparently, the adhesive on my heated handlebar grip no longer

adheres to the throttle and just moves around ineffectually. "Leave it with me for an hour and you'll be good to go," he says.

After killing an hour reading in Macdonalds around the corner, I thank Phil profusely. Epoxy resin and wire having fixed the problem, he asks for $20 but I give him $50. And thinking myself lucky the problem arose so close to a bike shop and promising myself to try and learn a bit more about mechanics (though something as simple as glue would never have occurred to me) I twist the fixed throttle and head for Adelaide once more.

In a roadhouse south of Port Pirie I have a bad coffee just to escape for a while from the huge wind gusts outside. On the TV they announce that Scott Morrison is the new Prime Minister, "Strewth," says the owner eloquently, "that's seven in eleven years. Worse than fuckin' Italy!"

To be honest, it's not the best day on the road I've ever had. As the wind buffets me, a forest of wind turbines appears on a ridge to the west. Whoever built them certainly did their homework. I'm not too impressed with Port Wakefield, which seems to exist solely to service the Highway.

I'm soon, once again in the thick of rush hour traffic, this time Adelaide's. I glance into the cars and wonder at the driver's lives; each in their own bubble. Pulling over, I punch my destination into the GPS and manage to snap the end off the power cord, rendering it useless. Fuck! At the next servo, a trucker, noticing my plight, directs me to an electrical retailer just off the Highway and I'm soon sorted. Isn't civilization wonderful? I don't mind dueling with the mad Friday arvo traffic, as the dulcet female tones of my GPS confidently directs me through the leafy city, to friend of a friend Hamish's house in the forested Adelaide Hills.

Motorcycle Journo
Hamish Cooper

Riding motorcycles has been a passion of Hamish's since his school days, when the movie *Easy Rider* hit the big screen and choppers were in vogue. "In Palmerston North in New Zealand, where I grew up, we'd get excited reading three-month-old issues of Motorcycle Mechanics from the UK."

His first bike, purchased in 1971 was a 1967 Triumph 3TA which he bought off another student. "There were basically two camps; Triumphs or Hondas," he says. "We'd call Honda riders, 'plastics' after the waterproof jackets they'd where. We were far too cool for that and wore army great coats."

Hamish used his primarily British bikes for commuting, to Polytechnic where he studied Journalism in Wellington and later to jobs on mainstream newspapers in Nelson and then Australia. He went from reporter to sub-editor in newspapers, then through the ranks of newspaper production to running magazines. "For most of my career I worked for News Ltd," he says.

Hamish and his family moved here from Sydney where he worked on the Mirror. "A big factor were the magnificent motorcycling roads here in the Adelaide hills. I'd fly away a lot on assignments and flying back, I'd gaze down at these hills, knowing that in 30 minutes I could be on my bike enjoying them. Living in Melbourne and Sydney, it might take you an hour to get to a good road, but here it's literally on your doorstep. Dirt or bitumen, it's all right here."

Hamish grew up in an era when you'd simply take your road bike onto the dirt. "I remember when the first purpose-built dirt bike came on the market," he says. "They called the BMW R80 GS, the two wheeled Range Rover but if you ever rode them, you'd realise what a piece of junk they were. A mate of mine rode one from the UK over to here about 15 years ago and he hated it!"

I ask Hamish how working for a newspaper worked. What was the process? "Well, working for mainstream newspapers, you'd get different rounds. It might be on the Court rounds or the Police rounds or Education, things like that. When I became a sub-editor, I'd have to make sure the reporter's stories were fit for publication. I'd have to shorten them and write the headlines. I'd work on the Sport sections or the Feature sections or Finance sections."

While doing this he'd write for Motorcycle magazines in his spare time. Then during a trip to the Isle of Man in the late 80's he met some journalists who asked Hamish if he'd like to write some stories on Australian motorcycling and feature stories on particular bikes. "And that's how my motorcycling writing career started really, though it was a second job at first."

When News Ltd decided to have a re-shuffle of the motoring section, Hamish became the main motorcycle journalist for a few years, mixing work with pleasure, a thing most people only dream of. He'd get to test ride new models and attend bike launches. "Sounds like the perfect job and of course I enjoyed it, but it was relentless. If I went to a bike launch in Spain for instance, I'd spend more time flying there than being there. Then, I'd arrive jet lagged and have to jump on a sports bike and go howling around a race track. It does sound glamourous, but it soon loses its gloss."

Hamish reckons that bike launches have changed a lot since he started doing them in the mid 90's. "Suddenly you'd get these so-called journalists show up who were actually former Grand Prix champions. People like Niall Mackenzie who is severely fast on a race track. You'd be on an R1 going at a reasonable clip and they'd come whizzing past you. And of course, today you see lots of stunt riding because magazines want pictures of wheelies and stoppies which I really can't relate to."

I tell Hamish I'm in complete agreement and confess that I've never done a wheelie in my life! But that is the beauty of motorcycling, in that there are many sub-cultures. Viva la difference! Some like to get their knee down on the track, some like to dirt and mud. Some like polishing their chrome and cruising at high speed on the highway. Others like the feeling of grease under their finger nails as they tinker around with engines in their man-cave. "But you asked me earlier why I got into motorcycling, and I suppose one word sums it up: Freedom," he says. "I also love working on bikes, fixing up old ones and restoring them."

Hamish comes from the era when you had to learn to fix things for yourself. "You'd be told, 'I'm only going to show this once,' so you learned to listen. There's actually a sub-culture starting now in places like Melbourne and Sydney, where communal workshops are springing up. Places where you can take your bike and be taught how to maintain it and fix it. So that's the kind of old school thing that I grew up with. Also, in the 70's a lot of shops refused to work on Triumphs, Nortons or BSA's, so you'd have to have a go yourself. They were transitioning to Japanese bikes and basically the British bikes had had their day."

Hamish writes a regular column for Australian Motor Cycle News called, "Old School" where he waxes lyrically about the motorcycling scene of the 70's and 80's. He says, "One of the magazine's young designers told me he wished he'd grown up in that era as I made it sound so cool. But it was a great time to be a motorcyclist."

Writing for magazines has allowed Hamish to tour on bikes in some fascinating parts of the world, such as South Africa, Morocco and the Adriatic Coast. "It's on these trips that I met fellow motorcyclists my age and you realise that we're all getting older. So, the challenge is in how to get younger people involved in motorcycling. It seems to have jumped a generation, with people in their twenties getting into it but heaps of 30 or 40 somethings out there who seemed to have no interest."

Hamish, like myself, prefers to ride alone but does belong to the Ducati Owners Club and the Historic Racing Register. He plans to go for a ride with the Ducati club this coming Sunday. "The best times I've ever had on a motorcycle have been just me on the road alone," he says. "Motorcycling is dangerous. Of course, it is. To become a good rider, you must do a lot of it, so it becomes intuitive. You may be coming into a corner too hot and a lot of people will panic. But with experience you stay calm and rely on your skills, look where you want to go and simply lean over more and gently accelerate out of trouble. It seems to take a lot more effort to just jump on your bike these days but it's something you've got to keep up and make yourself do it regularly." He also does track days occasionally as well as bit of dirt riding, saying it's good to mix it up.

These days, Hamish works freelance and is also the news editor for Australian Motor Cycle News but points out that he's semi-retired. Working with different photographers, he identifies interesting bikes or people worth doing a feature on and sells the article to various magazines around the world. "For example, a few years ago, I did a piece on how the Britten motorcycles were rescued from the Christchurch earthquakes, a story I was surprised nobody had thought to do."

Hamish takes me into his workshop/office/man cave where he writes and works on his bikes. He apologises for the mess but I think it's quite tidy and has a great vibe. Inside are his 1986 Yamaha IT 200 Enduro, his 1948 Triumph Tiger which he and a friend built from a stack of parts, a lovely 1974 850 Norton Commando and under a sheet, his Ducati which he plans to ride with me for a while tomorrow.

Chapter Nine.

INTO THE MORNING SUN

*"I'm a man of means, by no means,
king of the road."*

Roger Miller

Checking my emails in the morning, I notice one from Canberra giving me only a small window of opportunity to interview a certain VIP there. There am I, banging on about the freedom of the road, etc. and I've made myself a slave to the clock! Unfortunately, I won't now have time to take up Hagen Stehr's offer to visit his Maritime and Fisheries Academy, or indeed his daughter Yasmin's 'swimming with tuna' facility and I feel a bit guilty after the kindness and hospitality they showed me.

But again, my mood lifts as I ride behind Hamish through the beautiful Adelaide Hills on magic, twisty roads that must have been engineered by a biker, through quaint old towns, vineyards and farmland. At the servo, I remind him that I'm riding a KLR and nod towards his stunning 2006 Ducati Sport Classic, a 992cc beast capable of 217 kph. But I needn't have worried for Hamish is content to cruise along and smell the roses.

We wind down to Wellington on the Murray River and cross Australia's longest river (2,508 kilometres) on a free punt that runs 24

hours a day. This mighty water highway is part of the Murray-Darling river system, whose catchment area is one-seventh of Australia's colossal landmass.

At Meningie, set on the shores of the picturesque Lake Albert, Hamish leaves me and with a wave, returns to his life. I'm now on the Pacific Highway, the same long road that passes by my old house in Sydney. I allow Percy to lift up his skirts and kick up his heels (he's a crossdresser) as I open the throttle a bit, breath in the sea air and indulge in some faster riding, with the sheltered saltwater lagoons of the Coorong National Park immediately to my right. The 47,000-hectare park is a birdwatcher's paradise with 240 species recorded in the area. After 145 kilometres of near bliss, I arrive in the strangely named Kingston S.E. on the shores of Lacepede Bay. Just up the road from a 17-metre-tall, steel and fibreglass sculpture of Larry the Lobster, I sip my coffee. A little girl with blonde curls at the next table asks me if I'm her friend Lucy's grand-dad. When I smile and shake my head, she asks me how old I am and when I tell her I'm 59, her eyes go wide, and she says, "my daddy's only 37!" When her dad stops laughing, he warns me that there are a lot of 'roos between here and Mt Gambier 150 odd kilometres south.

I soon discover the truth in his warning, as twice in the afternoon 'roos jump across the road, thankfully way ahead of me. Through Mt Gambier and into Victoria, the Princes Highway delivers me to

the charming and popular holiday destination of Port Fairy. This picture-postcard town has a proud seafaring history, with lobster, abalone and squid boats still operating. I'm soon booked into the charming YHA Hostel, a favourite of mine I've stayed in a couple of times before.

I wake up, yawn and scratch my balls. For a couple of seconds, I feel disoriented. My leather jacket, helmet, boots and panniers lie at the foot of my bed in a tiny bedroom. Then the penny drops, and it all comes back to me. Today I'm excited for I'm riding perhaps the most iconic ribbon of tarmac in the Antipodes, The Great Ocean Road, a ride I'd done three or four years back on a BMW hire bike for an article in *New Zealand Bike Rider Magazine*.

You may be surprised to read that the famous GOR is only 244 kilometres long. It's an easy day's ride but a lot of tourists take their time and spin it out, as there are plenty of diversions. It hugs the coastline, crosses rugged headlands, passes green farmland and bisects towering forests. The Australian-National-Heritage-listed GOR was built by returned-soldiers between 1919 and 1932 and is, in effect, the world's largest war memorial, dedicated as it is to the fallen of World War 1.

The day is cool and cloudy, with rain predicted for later. Through mixed farmland, I'm soon in Warrnambool. Originally a whaling and sealing station, it's now home to 30,000 people. I stop Percy by

the whale viewing platform, where southern right whales can sometimes be viewed as they give birth. Not today though.

According to my free map, the GOR officially begins at Allansford, 12 kilometres along, where I look in vain for a decent café. I carry on to The Twelve Apostles car park, which is chock-full of Asian tourists, some grumbling about the five-minute walk under the highway to the viewing platforms. Dressed in high fashion, they play with their phones and grimace at the wind. I offer to take a photo of a family of four and I'm rewarded by far more smiles and bows than my assistance deserves. The Twelve Apostles really does live up to its billing and is probably the tourist highlight of the GOR. The magnificent 15-metre limestone stacks, lashed by the surf are quite a sight.

The rain comes as predicted around noon, and I ride under an awning just in time to suit up. From Princetown, the GOR (also known as the B 100), heads inland through the forested Otway National Park and I quickly become reacquainted with riding on twisty, wet roads with wet leaves on corners and incompetent Sunday drivers.

I park up opposite the perfect crescent of sand that makes up Apollo Bay and head for the coffee shop. Wordsmith, Rudyard Kipling was very impressed with Apollo Bay, describing it as 'paradise.' I peel myself out of my wet weather gear and enjoy afternoon eggs and bacon, while making another puddle on the floor. Instinctively (and I'm not an ex-spy or anything cool like that) I like to sit with my back to the wall, facing the street if possible. I read somewhere that the only time Wild Bill Hickock broke his own golden rule and sat with his back to the door, he got shot. The young girl who brings my coffee tells me she's checked her phone and the rain is over, bless her cotton socks.

A dry and sunny ride to Torquay dries out my wet gear. I lose count of the bends in the road. Storm damage and road works slow up traffic on an already slow road, but the sun is now shining, and the sea is sparkling on my right, so who cares? I make Geelong, Victoria's largest provincial city just as the sun is sinking, and book into the first little motel near the city centre. After a frugal meal of left-overs from my small larder, I fall asleep on a huge bed, watching President Trump make an idiot of himself once more on CNN.

There's no avoiding next morning's ride, as I have to skirt the behemoth of Melbourne in order to get to Gippsland and continue east. Not sure of my destination, I punch in the address of a Hostel in Foster into my GPS and head off. I thought I'd managed to avoid the predicted shower, but as the skyline of Melbourne emerges, it starts to drizzle. I'm now stuck between five lanes of steel and plastic with nowhere to pull over to waterproof my GPS. I then realise I've made a mistake by pressing, 'yes' to avoiding toll roads. I'm not that much of a tight-arse, it's just that I'd been given such a frustrating run-around when attempting to pay a couple of toll roads fees from Sydney that I knew if I had to face those telephone conversations again, I would go insane. I shouldn't have been surprised, therefore, after riding over a magnificent bridge crossing the Yara, to be directed into the morning's rush hour traffic, onto Power Street in the heart of Melbourne's City Centre. And of course, it's now started to properly rain. I perform a dodgy 'U' turn, narrowly avoid being sideswiped by a hooting bus, pull onto a pavement full of busy pedestrians who have to walk around me, and re-set the GPS, taping a Ziploc bag over it. I've now got heavy rain, a fogged-up visor and wet tram lines to contend with. But for some perverse reason, I can't help but smile and shaking my head, start singing Pearl Jam's *Even Flow* at the top of my lungs.

I eventually shake off Melbourne's sprawl and find myself back on the M1 heading east as the rain stops. I manage somehow to glide between huge dark clouds pregnant with rain, into the blue. The Highway is excellent but it's a bit too excellent really. While it might improve the GDP by oiling the wheels of industry, it does nothing for a road trip. It's all just too easy and although I'm eating up the miles, it kind of detracts from my journey. So, it's a relief when the Motorway turns into the old Princes Highway, complete with human-scale things like road works, small towns and oncoming traffic.

In the Latrobe Valley, I pass the huge Loy Yang Power Station, fuelled by locally-mined brown coal. The two sections, Loy Yang A and B represent the largest power station in Australia, providing 50% of Victoria's requirements.

I park Percy in Sale's pedestrian mall and after a walk around the good-sized High Street in the sun, have a well-earned coffee and sandwich. Despite my impressions to the contrary, the lady at the next table tells me that this area is quite depressed economically and if it wasn't for the RAAF having its main base here, there wouldn't be much work. She has an exceptionally loud voice, so assuming she's a bit deaf, I raise mine a notch too.

It's a cold and windy ride through East Gippsland's heavily forested hills, with Lakes Wellington, Victoria and King between me and the sea. Apart from my break in Sale, I've been in the saddle since 7.30 so I'm more than happy to book into a very comfortable room at the Lakes Entrance RSL. I buy a warm sweater at the op shop next door for four dollars. "You're the third person today to buy a warm jumper," says the grey-haired lady behind the counter, "people forget it's winter down here." Warmly clad, I stroll along the picturesque marina and admire the commercial fishing vessels and pleasure boats. Later, I join a happy host of holiday-makers in the RSL and consume a seafood platter that would have fed a whole family.

The clear morning skies are under siege from a huge grey and black cloud-bank on the horizon. Long tendrils of rain, like spider webs, seem to hang from the clouds in the distance. I've got so many layers on that I can barely walk to my bike. As I head up into the misty hills the rain comes down in earnest. Some great photos of the giant eucalypts around the town of Orbost go unclicked as the

effort involved in stopping and getting my camera out in the wet is just too much. I pass many rest areas tucked into the forest, which would be an attractive proposition if it were dry. The iconic gum, or eucalyptus tree (I defy you to imagine a vision of the Aussie bush without one) was, according to fossil plant evidence, quite rare here 50,000 years ago. With the arrival of Homo Sapiens and their practice of fire agriculture, the fire-resistant eucalyptuses survived and over the next few thousand years, spread where other species went extinct.

Percy and I are suddenly graced with a couple of rays through the murk but it's a false dawn. Starving hungry, cold, wet and low on petrol, I interrupt my journey, stopping at the cool little town of Cann River, which emerges out of the murk and has a real frontier vibe. The little settlement has an old, country feel to it. The old lady who serves me eggs on toast smiles and almost pats me on the head, so concerned is she by my damp demeanour. "It's cleared up in New South Wales love," she assures me. And sure enough, the rain miraculously stops, as later on, I cross into New South Wales. The realisation that the end of my journey is in sight is a sobering one.

Eden is one of my favourite little towns and one I'd often ridden down to from Sydney. In the forecourt of the servo, I investigate the rattling noise that's been bugging me for a while. My chain is knackered. It's so stretched that attempts to adjust it don't help, but I figure it will get me to Sydney. As I tinker, my gear strewn all over the forecourt, a tanker driver from Manchester, delivering 49,000 litres of 91 octane unleaded petrol, pauses to talk football. He supports United, I support City. "But you're a Londoner!" he says. I shrug. It's a long story. I tell him that Spurs beat United 3-0 last night. "Thanks a lot," he says, "I've recorded that game and now I know the score." Whoops! A stream of colourful invective follows but he's got a smile on his face. "Anyway mate, safe riding," he sighs as he climbs into his cab, "the sun's shining all the way to Bateman's Bay."

Eden is a deep-water port and tourist hub with a long history (for Australia) based on the whaling industry, which flourished between

1818 and the 1930s. The late 19th-century gold rush also played a part when the shiny stuff was discovered in nearby Kiandra, Eden being the nearest port. I visit the Killer Whale Museum, a nicely laid out establishment where I gaze at the skeleton of 'Old Tom', the killer whale. Apparently, Tom and his pod would herd baleen whales into Twofold Bay and alert whalers on shore by bashing the water with their tails (flop-tailing).

Passing large herds of dairy cows, mostly Jerseys, I park at the kerb on the main drag for a delicious al-fresco lunch as happy, well-heeled tourists and locals wander by. From my seat, I can see smoke, far off above the hills, evidence of recent forest fires.

The 150 kilometres of road between Bega and Bateman's Bay is one of the best biking roads in the country. I smile to myself. Put simply, at the moment, I am a happy little bunny. Some politicians are calling to replace Gross Domestic Product, the accepted yardstick for a nation's success (but in reality, a barometer of Corporation's profits) with GDH or Gross Domestic Happiness. As Yuval Noah Harari says in his thought-provoking book, Homo Deus, "After all, what do people want? They don't want to produce. They want to be happy. Production is important because it provides the material base for happiness. But it is only the means, not the end." You have to ask yourself, in a world of super-abundance, why are so many in the so-called first world killing themselves. Buddha suggested that to attain real happiness we should slow down our relentless pursuit of pleasant sensations, not accelerate it. As I transfer my gear into the dormitory of the Batemans Bay YHA hostel, my blood still fizzing, I wonder what Buddha would have made of riding a motorcycle on such a wonderful road. It's a short walk into town, where I treat myself to fish 'n' chips, swimming in salt and vinegar.

I share the eight-bed dorm room with a young cray fisherman called James, who constantly nips outside to smoke, douses himself liberally in a pungent aftershave and unfortunately snores like a train. Also, at the hostel is a young German girl from Berlin in a hire car and a grey-haired nurse from Bega, attending a seminar on elderly abuse in rest homes. "I have to do at least 20 hours of personal

development a year to stay registered," she tells me in a tiny voice I can barely hear. As I lean closer to hear her (my industrial deafness doesn't help) she recoils as though slapped, before recovering. "It's a very relevant course," she whispers, "as this area is retiree's heaven."

Captain Cook named the bay during his historic journey up the east coast in 1770 but gave no reason for his name choice. Batemans Bay is a prosperous and popular town, not just with retirees but with holidaymakers, many of whom descend from Canberra at weekends as this is the capital's closest seaside town.

Ignoring Buddha's suggestion to slow down my pursuit of pleasant sensations, I enjoy more fantastic riding the next day as I leave the coast and ride over the Great Dividing Range towards Canberra. I can take my time as it's only a short ride of 150 kilometres or so. There has been no expense spared on this road. The Kings Highway is a superb feat of engineering, twisting and turning through the hills as it takes me inland to the lovely old bush town of Braidwood for coffee in a cool, converted coach-house. As I sip, a guy reads out a newspaper article to his partner. Apparently (he tells her) Madame Tussauds in Sydney has stopped work on ex-Prime Minister Malcolm Turnbull's wax figure as the museum's curators wonder if it's worthwhile adding any more Australian PMs to its world leaders exhibit.

Just out of Braidwood my mood of pleasant melancholia is interrupted as I round a bend. There's so much roadkill, it resembles a war zone. First with dead wombats and then seven or eight 'roos that must have been hit en-masse like dominoes in a big bloody lump. I also see the first dead koalas of the trip. As the trees wilt in the continuing dry spell (all of NSW is now officially in drought), the leaves become less nutritious and the koalas leave the safety of the trees to forage, leaving them at risk from vehicles as well as dogs. The bush is bone dry again, a dryness I haven't seen since the Nullarbor.

The modern YHA Hostel in Canberra is huge and located right in the CBD, surrounded by tall buildings and construction sites. I park Percy around the back and ferry my gear in the elevator, up to my eight-bed dorm. One top bunk is occupied by a peroxide blonde American woman of around 40. She's tucked up in bed at two in the afternoon with her nose stuck in a book. "Oh, hi!" she says without preamble and her eyes shining, "I think I've found the salvation of my soul," and indicates her weighty tome. "I'm converting to the Russian Orthodox Church," she gushes, "and I'm a Mormon for goodness sake!"

I wonder if she's mistaken me for someone else – someone well-versed with her situation. She continues breathlessly as I put my gear away and make my bed, "I never want to set foot in the US ever again! My heart's broken but I think I've finally found the answer." I'm almost lost for words but manage, "well I'm very pleased for you."

"It's all in here, you see," she says, holding the book up to me as though I'm supposed to immediately share in her enlightenment. I smile and mumble an apology as I must be on my way. As I head out the door her head is back in her book. I see her occasionally over the next three days around the Hostel, holding forth earnestly with other hostellers, some of whom seem to have acquired the old 1000-yard stare.

It's a pleasant walk up nearby Anzac Parade to the magnificent War Memorial for my next interview. Inside, everything is spick and span, making me feel a tad under-dressed in jeans and leather jacket. After being issued with an ID card which I wear around my neck, I'm ushered upstairs into the inner sanctum.

The Director.
Dr Brendan Nelson

I'm comfortably seated on a leather sofa in Brendon Nelson's plush and tastefully appointed office. Sitting opposite me is the man himself, well-groomed and dapper and looking in pretty good nick for a man of similar vintage to myself. He's a very down to earth and modest chap despite his above-average CV. Melbourne born, he was a General Practitioner in Hobart between 1985 and '95 and during this period was also Federal President of the Australian Medical Association. He then served as a Member of the House of Representatives as the Liberal member for the Division of Bradfield in North Sydney between 1996 and 2009.

And as if that were not enough, he served in two Howard Governments as Minister for Education, Science and Training and Minister of Defence, becoming the leader of the Liberal Party and Federal leader of the Opposition In 2007.

Brendon retired from Politics in 2009 when the then Prime Minister Kevin Rudd appointed him Ambassador of Australia to the EU, Belgium and Luxembourg, as well as the country's special representative to NATO.

I promise not to ask any political questions and instead, ask him how he got into motorcycling. Not surprisingly, he's a good talker. "I was doing an economics degree in Adelaide and I'd dropped out. It really wasn't for me," he begins. He'd later return to higher education at Flinders University to complete his Bachelor of Medicine and Surgery.

"So basically, I needed transport," he continues. "My father, who was a Marine Chief Steward, working for the National Australian Line asked around on his ship and managed to lay his hands on a reconditioned Honda CB 750 Four."

"That's not a bad start!" I say for the classic 750, upon introduction was called, 'the most sophisticated production bike ever,' by the influential Cycle magazine. Feeling that it was a bit much for a beginner, Brendon took the 750 to the local Honda dealer and swapped it for a brand new and more manageable CB 400 Four, also known as the CB400F, on which he learned to ride.

"Today the motorcycle test is a lot more difficult to the one I took back in 1976. As it should be," says Brendon. "A Police car followed me around for 15 minutes and said, 'yep, you're fine,' and that was that. But how I wished I knew back then what I know today!"

Brendon's assistant comes in with two cups of tea and as we sip, we talk bikes, of which he has owned a huge variety. Everything from four Honda 350 Four's ("loved the smooth little motor") to a Kawasaki 500 triple ("rip your arms off in the first two gears") to a Ducati 900SS Darmah ("wished I still owned it") to a white 2008 Suzuki Hayabusa. Apart from having a brief hiatus from motorcycling when his kids were young, he had been a regular rider since 1976.

"I'd loved riding all kinds of bikes throughout those years," he says, "from commuters to cruisers and racers. But I turned 60 recently and realised, especially in this job that there can be things worse than death. If I get killed on a bike, it won't worry me because I'll be dead. But if I spent three months in Intensive Care and years in Rehab – well that's not what I want. Obviously, I'm not critical of people who choose to ride as it's incredibly enjoyable and exhilarating. As you know George, unless you're an idiot, the risks in motorcycling are not from yourself. They're the other road users." I nod as I can't dispute the logic.

"And in Australia, of course, it's the wildlife," I add and it's Brendon's turn to nod. "Yeah, if you hit a wombat or kangaroo at speed on a bike, you're history. I've had a couple of near-misses myself over the years. So, I'd just reached the point where I thought, I'll quit while I'm in front."

Recently, while returning from the funeral of a close friend, where Brendon had once more read the eulogy, his wife asked him what he'd do if she suddenly passed away. "Well, God forbid, of course, I'd be devastated, and grief-stricken," he replied. "But what would you do after that?" she asked.

"I think I'd put a Hayabusa and a Triumph Thruxton in the living room, just to gaze at them, while I was having a beer and watching TV." He explains, "people pay big money for beautiful sculptures and paintings so they can sit there and appreciate them so why not look at motorcycles, which are such superb works of art?" Why not indeed, I think but feel I must change the subject, or we'll talk about bikes for the whole interview. Excusing my ignorance and lack of research I ask about his current job.

"Well, George if you were a Year 6 student, I'd liken being the Director of the War Memorial to being the Principal of the School. I'm the overall manager of the Memorial, responsible for the strategic direction of the place. We have a Council to which I report, but I'm responsible for the day to day, year to year running of the place and I drive a lot of the ideas that support the vision for the Memorial."

"Wow, that was a concise answer!"

He smiles, "I also see myself as an Ambassador for it, as I travel quite a bit, speaking publicly about the institution and what it means."

"So, you enjoy it?"

"Yes. It's a labour of love. When I was an Ambassador in Europe, I spent a lot of time visiting the various cemeteries and war memorials and that was what I appreciated the most. I remember telling my wife that when I returned to Australia, I wanted to do something meaningful. I knew I had more public service in me but didn't quite know what. When I saw the position of Director advertised, I knew it was for me. I went through the process and landed the job."

Brendon completed his initial term and was asked by the Government to sign on for another five years. He decided to sign on for another further two, which he plans to review towards the end of 2019. "I've found that it's usually best to leave things when people want you to stay," he says, which I find an interesting concept.

As Director, Brendon and his staff have been very busy recently with the 100th anniversary of the end of the First World War only weeks away. Many displays, exhibitions, projects, plays and social media programmes are planned. Among the displays will be 62,000 hand knitted poppies on kebab sticks with green sleeves spread all around the War Memorial grounds. There will be a lightscape that will sweep over them at night with a classical music soundscape as accompaniment. "And on the evening of the 10th November," says Brendon, "there will be a light beam that goes from the parapet of the Memorial to Parliament to emphasise the relationship and symmetry between the freedoms that are exercised and those that have paid for it."

And on November 11th an exhibition will open called After the War, which will explore the human, social and political consequences of war and what happens when it ends. This will feature many personal and emotional accounts of wars from World War 1 up to Afghanistan. There will also be a poignant photographic exhibition featuring First World War German war memorials and cenotaphs, of which, Brendon points out, there are surprisingly few.

"We're also producing a music CD. Garth Porter, the Kiwi keyboard player who founded the band Sherbet in the '70s has been making music with a good friend of mine, Lee Kernaghan for the past 20 years. And they've just completed an album called After the War, which they've kindly handed over to us. So, we've funded the production of it with some donations I've collected. A whole range of Australian artists perform on it and the royalties come back to us."

We talk country music for a while and I mention my interview with John Williamson, a singer Brendon has met and is, like me, a big fan of. We both agree that, like Lee Kernighan, there is far more to their songs than just country. "I've always loved country music," Brendon says, "Slim Dusty and his wife were actually at my wedding. And Slim told me that he didn't actually like his two biggest hits, A Pub with No Beer and Duncan. But Slim did some beautiful stuff around Henry Lawson's poetry."

Brendon confesses that he's not a fan of Hip Hop, Rap, Opera or Classical music but his tastes are quite eclectic, ranging from the country, classic rock and folk, to Dame Kiri te Kanawa and Pink. He's also, like me, a big fan of singer-songwriter Kris Kristofferson.

I ask him what he's reading at the moment. "What book is sitting on your bedside table?"

"Actually, I'm reading Charles Bean's The Western Front Diaries," he says. "He was our official World War 1 correspondent, who landed with our troops at Gallipoli and stayed with them throughout the entire war. He wrote copious diaries and later drew on the diaries to write and edit the twelve volumes that became the official history. And we at the War Memorial are publishing this new book, edited by Peter Burness next month. So, I've been reading an advanced copy."

Brendon says he can't be bothered with Crime novels, etc as he can watch them on TV, preferring to read historical novels or biographies. And speaking of TV, he loves the BBC police dramas such as Spooks but reckons the most entertaining shows he's ever seen on

TV were Breaking Bad and Band of Brothers. "My son put me on to Breaking Bad," he says. "It's one of those shows that you're going to love it or hate it after the first episode. But I've watched the whole series three times and the twists and turns are amazing. The fundamental message in the show is that every single person involved in the drugs business loses. Believe it or not, it has some very strong moral themes."

Forgetting my earlier promise, I ask Brendon if he misses politics and he doesn't have to think too much before replying. "No, I don't. I miss some of the people that I worked with. I had my turn and I made the most of some wonderful opportunities and left on my own terms with no regrets. I've enjoyed everything I've done in my life and I'm a great believer in looking forward and never going back."

"Is there anything you would have done differently?"

"Sure, there are little things I might have done differently but as far as career choices go, I wouldn't change a thing. I've enjoyed everything I've done. I said earlier that there are worse things than death and if I died tomorrow, I think people would say, 'he did the best he could and squeezed as much out of it as he could.'"

Finally, I ask Brendon what he thinks of the current political shenanigans in Canberra. He ponders this one for a bit. "There are existential questions about the future of Democracy – the way our respective nations work. But I think the changing of elected Prime Ministers by both sides that we've seen in the past decade is very damaging and the price is being paid by the nation itself. We as a people seem to have lost the capacity to have political leadership that delivers the reform necessary for our country to prosper and grow."

I don't know when these small mixed dorm rooms became popular, but these days they seem, like free Wi-Fi, to be taken for granted by backpackers. I must admit to feeling a bit self-conscious, trying to climb up into the swaying top bunk with as much grace as possible in my undies and T-shirt. I have my earplugs ready under my pillow in case somebody snores but thankfully, my fellow sleepers prove to be as quiet as church mice.

The same cannot be said for the half-pissed scouse girl who for some reason sits just outside the door, shrieking into her cell phone for the next half hour. Her Liverpool accent is so thick that at first, I think she's speaking Norwegian. She gives the game away when she says, "I was foockin' made-up like!" Thankfully she's sleeping in another room.

After a quick breakfast at the downstairs café, I set out with my day pack, leaving my roommates still sleeping. Central Canberra is easy to navigate with plenty of parkland, but seems to be devoid of any real centre or High Street. All life seems to gravitate to a giant, interconnected shopping mall. Everyone seems busy. Our society seems increasingly to value busyness over everything else. Busyness is something to aspire to. Busy people wear their busyness like a badge of honour. What they're really doing is telling others what high-status people they must be to be in such demand. Busy people make me feel tired. They're suffering from FOMO, or Fear of Missing Out, where people can't pay attention to one thing because they are always tempted by a myriad of different choices.

An air-conditioned mall is quite literally an anathema to me. Next time you're in one, look upon the expressions of your fel-

low shoppers. To me, they have the aspect of hunted, stressed-out prey. They swim in an ocean of abundance, most of it unnecessary. Everything is artificial, the air, the ground, the sky-starved light, the aromas. It's as though people are compelled by some alien force to consume processed food and drink, and to buy things they don't need and can ill afford. My blood pressure returns to normal levels however when I discover a huge Dymocks bookstore.

Canberra is very obviously a planned city, as many capitals are. It's pleasant enough to wander around on a sunny day but lacks that indefinable thing called character, which only age and natural development bring. My fellow pedestrians braving the outside world are mostly office workers, be-suited and clutching their devices and takeaway coffees, with a couple of homeless people pushing supermarket trolleys and few tourists in the mix. The city just seems to be too big for its population, as though it were awaiting the imminent arrival of thousands more residents.

I spend the afternoon exploring the War Memorial. Conceived by Charles Bean and opened in 1941, it was voted by travellers in 2016 as the number one landmark in the Trip Advisor Awards. The grand Byzantine-style sandstone building really is a sight, surrounded by clipped lawns and eucalypts and the whole thing is quite moving. I ignore my golden rule of Aussie riding that night and ride out in the dark to the inner suburb of Hughes where Martin, my last interviewee says he has pizza and beer waiting for me.

Iron Butt Rider
Martin Little

Martin's wife Rebecca plonks three large pizzas on the table and tells me to get stuck in, while Martin opens a can of VB for me. His entreaty to not stand on ceremony is unnecessary.

"My dad was into bikes and I remember as a kid, pouring over his black and white magazines," Martin, courtly and well mannered, begins. I don't have to ask him where he grew up because a few years back I'd interviewed his father Mike for my book, *Living The Dream*-Kiwi Bikers, in their family home in Wairoa on New Zealand's North Island. It was veteran biker Mike's suggestion that I interview his son for this book. "My brothers and my cousin all had bikes," continues Martin, "so from the age of 12 I'd be hopping on them for a ride. I passed my test at 15 on a small Honda I borrowed from a mate. It was your usual, casual small-town kind of test we had back in the day, where you're asked to ride up the road, do a figure eight and ride back."

In Wellington Martin completed his building cadetship while going through a wide range of motorcycles ranging from a Honda CB550K, a CB650, a CB750 Bol d'Or and a Yamaha XS1100 to a Suzuki GS850G shaft-drive, a lovely machine he rode all around the North Island. "That was one of the most comfortable bikes I've ever owned," he says, "but I sold it after it spat me off on the Motorway. They were renowned for having very sensitive steering heads. And once you have that doubt in your bike, it's never the same again."

After a bad accident riding his Honda 750 Bol d'Or, he was soon back in the saddle when a work colleague lent him his BMW R80 to take for a spin. Accustomed to smooth multi-cylinder engines, Martin initially thought the Beemer a piece of crap, but his mate suggested he take it up to the mid-winter Cold Kiwi Rally. "I was determined to get the monkey off my back," says Martin, "I'd either be back in the saddle or I'd stay out of it." After a weekend riding in snow, hail and rain, he realised that he was sold on BMW, a love affair that has lasted to this day.

We now get on to Martin's passion, some might say his obsession. For Martin belongs to a sub-culture of endurance riders that like to ride incredible distances in as little time as possible. Now residing in Canberra, Martin had his first long-distance adventure in 2007. "I was in my mid 40's and feeling burnt out so decided to ride around Australia. I rode to the coast, turned left and followed Highway One all around."

Unlike my trip, Martin chose one of the wettest winters the north had ever seen and was often cold and wet. His modus operandi differs from mine in that he is a very early riser and likes to hit the road, way before the sun had risen. To limit wildlife encounters, he'd always try to tuck in behind a road train.

"I normally get up at around 4am," says Martin, polishing off another piece of pizza. His wife and I exchange glances and laugh, agreeing that that just isn't normal. Martin had a great time, particularly appreciating the camaraderie of people on the road and completed his lap in five weeks. "My longest day was 1085 kilometres between Three Ways and Darwin," he says, "but I usually sat on around 120 kph because, anything above that, the BMW GS 1150 really started to drink the juice. It's all about managing your fatigue and your concentration levels: Finding the speed you're comfortable with. There is an Iron Butt Association certified ride around Australia called, "A Lap of the Big Paddock", which you must complete in under nine days," he says, "which I'm planning to do some time soon."

The Iron Butt Association (IBA) is an American based organisation with over 60,000 members worldwide, all dedicated to long-distance motorcycling. The minimum certified ride is the Saddle Sore 1000 –1000 miles (1600 kilometres) in under 24 hours. The first official Iron Butt Rally took place in 1984 with only 10 riders but has gradually grown to the international corporate event it is today. The endurance rides are many and various, but the Iron Butt Rally represents the Holy Grail, a riding marathon of 11,000 miles in 11 days, each event taking in different points of interest around the continental USA. In the 2017 Rally, 89 riders finished from a starting field of 107. Bob Higdon, poet laureate of the IBA and no slouch himself in the riding department, calls these long-distance bikers, 'the last cowboys.'

Martin has completed three Saddle Sore 1000's here in Australia – Perth to Sydney in 50 hours on two occasions and Sydney-Perth-Sydney in 100 hours, once. Martin describes the official IBA Rally in the USA is a giant scavenger hunt or orienteering on bikes. "It's very tightly regulated and well organised," he explains. "To prove you've been to the designated points within the times, you take photos, ensuring that your rally flag is in the picture and keep receipts, stamped with the time and date."

To compete in the official Rally, you must provide a resume to prove that you are fit to participate, known as a, 'No Dickhead Policy' in IBA circles. "You must have the runs on the board," explains Martin, "the IBA is a privately-owned organisation run like a benevolent dictatorship, for want of a better description. But you have to know what you're doing as it's pretty serious and dangerous stuff."

Martin started his personal training regime about five years ago, regularly knocking off his own Saddle Sore targets, as well as completing a Butt Light Rally (no.7) in the States, which he just squeaked through. He reckons he came away from that one with his tail between his legs and basically discovered just how much he didn't know. He confirmed these rides with photos and receipts (some from ATM's at 'corner' points) and eventually received his official IBA Rally number 579, making him the 579th person to participate in the elite event. Martin completed his first Iron Butt Rally last year, riding a 2005 BMW RT 1200 which he bought, 'sight unseen' from a gentleman in Chicago.

"He had used the bike on the 2015 Rally and for various reasons, hadn't finished. But it was comfortable, well-fettled, with auxiliary fuel tank and cruise control and ready to go. There were five categories of bonus points to collect on the Rally, or the North American Safari, which was held over three legs and on each leg, the puzzles you had to solve would change. For instance, you had to ride to a farm in North Dakota and take a photograph of a statue of Gandalf the wizard. All the bonus point GPS locations are given to you on a thumb drive, while the puzzles you must solve are given on a word document. You get this information at 8 pm the night before, so you have study it and decide where you're going to go and then hopefully get some sleep."

Phew! I shake my head as I had no idea it was as complex and challenging as this. "And between your start and finish, you don't really know where you'll be going so you have to kind of sort yourself out on the fly," he adds.

Martin finished a very respectable 72nd out of a field of 110, which he was very happy with as his goal for his first Rally was merely to finish. I ask about speeding. "The IBA doesn't encourage speeding," he replies, "but you have to remember that culturally, there are no fixed speed cameras in America. You have Billy Bob with his speed gun which allows local Sherif's to raise revenue, but many people comfortably drive way in excess of the speed limit. And you have to remember George, that as an 'alien' caught speed-

ing, you can be thrown in jail."

Martin and Rebecca also completed the Iron Butt Light Rally this year two up. I ask Rebecca if she enjoyed the experience of being a pillion. "In hindsight, yes," she says, "but after the six days were up, one of the organisers asked if they'd see me back next year and I said, 'no way in hell!' I was fatigued and uncomfortable for the last couple of days, as the pillion seat on the R1200 RT was never designed for a pillion, if you like. Also, I need my eight hours sleep a night, whereas Martin could sleep and has slept behind a dumpster at the servo."

Rebecca is a motorcyclist in her own right and rides a Honda 800 crossover. She's not sure if she wants to ride the Iron Butt Rally solo but has been persuaded to join Martin as a two-up team for next year's event. I jokingly suggest that she should get into training immediately and go and sleep behind a skip!

We go to the garage, where I'm shown the couple's collection of immaculate bikes. "I've always been interested in just riding my bike," Martin sums up, "and I'll happily ride it from dawn till dusk."

It's time to leave and as usual, it's been a pleasure. As I hop on my bike and ride off down the road, Martin, half-man and half-motorcycle gives me a cheery wave from his front yard.

I get a new chain fitted next morning, despite the fact that I haven't got far to ride. I'm just a bit anal like that. "She was well and truly rooted!" the young mechanic with a wild tangle of hair tells me as he water-blasts all the oil, dust and accumulated shit from beneath the bike, which saves me a job as the bike must be spotless when it gets crated up again in Sydney. "We don't often get any trouble with these KLR's," he says, "they're like fuckin' tractors!"

Later, I wander the shores of Lake Burley Griffen, the artificial body of water at the geographic centre of Canberra. Completed after the damming of the Molongo River, it was named after Walter Burley Griffen, the American architect who won a competition in 1911 (ten years after Federation and the same year the ACT was proclaimed) to design Australia's capital. The Great Depression and World War 11 slowed the city's development considerably and the lake bearing his name and who's shore I now sit and eat a scotch egg on, was not completed until 1963. Before the name Canberra was chosen, some laughable suggestions were considered, like Wheatwoolgold, Sydmeladperbrisho and my personal favourite, Victoria Defendera Defender! Also on its shores can be found many hours of entertainment for the more cerebral or culturally inclined tourist in the form of Parliament House, the Australian National University, National Library, National Museum and National Gallery.

It's raining in the morning, so rather than get wet and miserable on Percy I decide to stay another night and get wet, walking to Parliament House, but I know I'm in denial and am just prolonging my trip by another day. My final ride next day is a formality really. With a sigh I clunk my faithful Kawasaki into gear and head for Sydney in bright sunshine to complete my lap. I could take the direct route up the Hume Highway but instead, I retrace my route back to Batemans Bay and up the coast. As I ride, I've plenty of time to reflect on the last eight weeks. The trip has given me the opportunity to simply observe without the ringing phone, the TV, the computer, the bright lights, endless aisles of plenty and the muzak of the supermarket. The insidious, intrusive, squawk of advertising, beseeching you to buy, to 'not miss out'. Conditions apply. Yes indeedy.

Henry Cole, presenter of World's Greatest Motorcycle Rides, said, "You have no concept, in normal life, of the loneliness you feel out on those roads. An old biker once said to me that loneliness breeds solitude and solitude breeds serenity. In that case, if you want to find serenity, ride around Australia."

It's hard for a big journey like this not to change you I suppose, even if the changes are very subtle. At times my motorcycle felt like a small boat on a land voyage through the bush. I think of the 16,000 kilometres of road that have flashed beneath my boots and realise what a lucky man I am as I've always felt most alive on the move.

Australia is a big nation with a big heart and will always hold a special place in mine. When I look at a map of Australia now, I, of course, conjure up memories of the big skies and awesome landscapes – but mostly I see the faces of the colourful characters who have shared their stories and laughter and often, their homes with me.

Australian country folk are resilient and stoic. Qualities they will need in the coming decades as our changing climate brings more severe flooding, drought, and bush fires. Experts even predict that parts of this huge country will become uninhabitable. And the growing rise in Nationalism throughout the world has once again given racists and bigots a voice, making the handling of immigrants and refugees more controversial than ever in the Lucky Country.

ACKNOWLEDGEMENTS

My heartfelt thanks to all the people I interviewed in this book, who were very generous with their time and in sharing their stories. It was a pleasure to make their acquaintance. Thanks also to Murray "Muzza" Olds in Sydney, Ken "Tuna Boy" Banwell in Ashburton, Fiona Baird and Lisa Devlin in Longreach, Tiffany Maynard in Karratha and Bill Mortlock and Nicky Hogarth in Christchurch for providing me with their details and suggesting I contact them. Thanks to Bill Honeybone for his efforts in trying to get this book published and to my fellow writer and motorcyclist Des Molloy for forming the publishing collective Kahuku and coming to the rescue when I thought it would never see the light of day.

And finally, special thanks to my wife Karen for encouraging me to head off on my bike alone. Allowing one another independence and freedom, is I think, the secret to a successful marriage.